SÖDERBLOM
ECUMENICAL PIONEER

SÖDERBLOM
ECUMENICAL PIONEER

By Charles J. Curtis

AUGSBURG PUBLISHING HOUSE

MINNEAPOLIS, MINNESOTA

SÖDERBLOM: ECUMENICAL PIONEER
Copyright © 1967 Augsburg Publishing House
All rights reserved
Library of Congress Catalog Card No. 67-11719

Manufactured in the United States of America

Dedicated to

NORMA

BETH

LINELL

SUSAN

Preface

The life and thought of the great ecumenical world church leader, theologian, and historian of religions, Archbishop Nathan Söderblom of Sweden, have attracted and fascinated Christian laymen, scholars, and clergy across denominational lines. Most of the studies of Söderblom have been either biographical or detailed discussions of certain phases of his thought. Few of these are presently available in English. There is no real survey of his work in theological perspective available to the English-speaking world, except my doctoral thesis published under the title *Nathan Söderblom: Theologian of Revelation.*

This present work is the first comprehensive and popular presentation of the basic facts of Söderblom's life and the major themes of his thought in the English language. The approach, with the exception of the biographical chapter, is systematic rather than historical. Only where the historical development of Söderblom's work and thought was essential to a proper understanding of the totality of his ecumenical vision has an effort been made to indicate crucial junctures in the evolution of his ideas. Thus the total picture of Söderblom's life and thought has been preserved intact for the reader to whom this book is the first introduction to one of the greatest ecumenical minds in the twentieth century.

It is especially important for the reader to note that the critical section is focused in Chapter VI. The writer faced two options in the structure of this book. One was to scatter the many salient criticisms of Söderblom throughout the book. The other was to focus all the criticisms in one chapter. The author chose the latter alternative.

The reason for this choice was twofold. First, the author felt the necessity to achieve the maximum clarity in exposition of the thought of Söderblom. The essential purpose of this book is to introduce the complex thought of Söderblom to the English-speaking world and to acquaint the reader with the vast scope of Söderblom's interests. Secondly, the author felt that in the interest of clarity and neatness it would be more valuable to sum up the criticisms in a single chapter. The reader who is not familiar with the vastness and complexity of Söderblom's thought would probably be confused with the introduction of criticisms in the expository chapters. Söderblom was an unsystematic genius similar to Luther. Therefore a special effort is required to organize and systematize his writings. The essential thrust of this book is to assist the reader in forming a clear picture of the life and thought of Söderblom and to understand his perennial contemporaneity.

C. J. Curtis

Chicago, Illinois

Contents

Picture Section: insert following page 54

CHAPTER I

SÖDERBLOM'S RELEVANCE TODAY

Archbishop Nathan Söderblom of Sweden is one of the most significant theologians and church leaders of the twentieth century. His creative ideas about the thought and practice of the Christian faith and the church are in some respects even more relevant in our time than when he lived during the first half of our century. Many of the problems which then were just germinating have now blossomed and mushroomed into full-grown movements, which pose a threatening challenge to the faith and work of the Christian and his church in the space age. As a consequence of these developments, Christianity has been pulled into the whirlpool of theological unrest and revolution, which is symbolized by (a) the rise of the God-is-dead theology, and (b) the secular city. Söderblom dimly envisaged the rise of these challenges to Christian faith and provided profoundly suggestive and relevant answers to the problem of the relationship between faith and culture, and the Gospel and modern man.

Söderblom, who died in 1931, could not have known the precise shape of "radical theology" which three decades later was to be propagandized by William Hamilton and Thomas J. J. Altizer. However, both Altizer and Hamilton reckon the German nineteenth-century philosophers Ludwig Feuerbach and Friedrich Nietzsche among their spiritual forebears. These two philosophers, in one form or another, proclaimed the death of God. Undoubtedly Söderblom learned of their ideas. The wide range of Söderblom's writings and the testimony of those who knew him and wrote accounts of his life and work (e.g., Tor Andrae, Bishop Eivind Berggrav, Archbishop Yngve Brilioth) afford ample evidence of his extraordinary sensitivity to the intellectual and cultural currents of his time. Nietzsche died in 1900 when Söderblom was writing his doctoral dissertation at

1

the Sorbonne while serving at the same time the Swedish congregation in Paris. Feuerbach, who died in 1872 when Söderblom was only six years old, laid the theoretical foundation for the dialectical materialism of Karl Marx (died 1883, the year Söderblom entered the University of Uppsala). Marxist Communism was a powerful force in Paris during the time when Söderblom was pastor there. If he had not already been familiar with the thought of Feuerbach, he certainly would have made its acquaintance through his contacts with Marxist, socialist, and communist ideology in the French capital or, later, with the Swedish socialist labor movement.

In relating Söderblom to the "secular city" theologians (Harvey Cox), the "secular meaning of the Gospel" school (P. M. Van Buren), the "God is dead" radicals (Wm. Hamilton and T. J. J. Altizer), and "religionless Christianity" (D. Bonhoeffer), no attempt is made to discuss the differences among these ideas and movements. I treat them as symptomatic expressions of the crisis of Christian faith in the twentieth century. My objective is to show forth the Söderblomian stance in relation to the modern crisis of Christianity, and thus to demonstrate his continuing relevance for theology and the church today. I am of course fully aware that Bonhoeffer's religionless Christianity, for example, is not identical with the "God is dead" theology of the 1960's in the U.S.A. It is not by accident, however, that theologians like Hamilton and Van Buren have seized upon the cryptic utterances of Bonhoeffer (made under pressure in various Gestapo prisons, and not at all characteristic of his main theological work) and used them extensively in their writings. Again, there are important differences between Cox and Hamilton, for instance. Hamilton views Cox's work on *The Secular City* as an attempt to popularize Barth (*Radical Theology and the Death of God*, p. 5.),[1] rather than to proclaim the death of God and to explore ways in which the Christian can still "make it as a Christian" after the event of the death of God. But a discussion of the differences (which, by the way, are, with the exception of Bonhoeffer, still subject to change) lies outside the purpose of the present work and will only confuse the reader primarily interested in Söderblom. I have therefore decided to omit references to the differences in the thought of these men.

GOD-IS-DEAD THEOLOGY

The unifying motif of the radical theology of some new theologians is that of "the death of God." For Archbishop Söderblom the unifying power of his life and thought was the living God. Nathan Söderblom was troubled and tormented by the recognition that in our time the reality of the transcendence of God has, for many, irretrievably lost its meaning and significance. He wrestled with this all-important question deeply and agonizingly in a manner similar to that of the contemporary God-is-dead theologians—men like Paul M. Van Buren, Thomas J. J. Altizer, and William H. Hamilton. And he found a way out of the difficulty into which he had been plunged by a loss of real transcendence. He found the living God who works through the process of reality, the God who continuously reveals himself in every true religion, the God who, as Paul said to the Greeks of Athens, at no time and nowhere has left himself without a witness. "I know that there is a living God," Archbishop Söderblom declared at the end of his life. "I can prove it by the history of religion."[2]

By a careful and scientific study of the history of all the major religions of the world, Söderblom became convinced that the decisive and characteristic element of all genuine religion is not the entertainment of a transcendent notion of a monotheistic God, but rather the sense of the holy. The new theologians of today are beginning to realize that the old, traditional, transcendental God concept can be dispensed with. Söderblom saw this quite clearly, but he insisted that there is one thing that is indispensable for all genuine religion, and that is what he termed "holiness." The essence of holiness does not depend on man so much as it depends on the divine influence of the overpowering rationality of divine self-revelation. The divine influence of holiness obliges man to strive for perfection. This striving implies obedience to the revelation of the good, and involves the urge to religious ideals and ethical perfection insofar as morality is implied by religion in the true and most profound sense of the word.

The incarnation and standard of holiness in Christianity is, for Söderblom, Jesus Christ. Some of the God-is-dead theologians have come to conclusions which are remarkably similar to the thought of Söderblom in this matter. It has come as a relief to men like Altizer that in the great crises of Christianity, which have shaken the foundations of the faith as they have never been shaken before, "Archbishop Söderblom judged the uniqueness of Christianity to lie in the fact that here revelation has the form of a 'man.' No word can be accepted as a Christian word which appears in an abstract, an inhuman or a nonhistorical form. To the extent that a word lies distant from a present and a human act of faith, or to the extent that it cannot become incarnate in the immediate horizon of faith—to that extent it must be judged to be non-Christian. Not non-Christian in an absolute or universal sense, of course, but rather non-Christian in the moment at hand, in the actual 'now' to which the Christian Word is directed."[3]

The insistence that Christianity must be empirically and contemporarily relevant has characterized the life and thought of Nathan Söderblom no less than the radical God-is-dead theology of the present time. The way of Christ's church in our time was, for him, the way of obedient service to Jesus. There was no doubt in the Archbishop's mind that the Jesus whom the New Testament proclaims can be known and available to us now with sufficient clarity to make his call to discipleship meaningful and compelling. The call to discipleship is the call to holiness as we see it lived by Jesus of Nazareth. Holiness is not merely an ethical word. Its main meaning for Söderblom is that of divine, "supernatural" power which in no way contradicts the empirical and pragmatic attitudes the Christian shares with his fellowmen in the modern world.

One of the strongest factors contributing to the rise of the God-is-dead theology has been the feeling that the old, traditional notions of Christianity have lost their relevance for the empirical bend of mind of modern man—indeed, they stand in direct and irreconcilable opposition to what men today know to be true and applicable to the human situation in the atomic and space age. There is a revulsion and rebellion against the other-worldliness of religion as it was "in the good old days," and a turning to what is relevant and practical in the secular pragmatism which characterizes American life and culture today. If the Word of God is really the incarnate

Word, it must also take human form in our culture, the culture of the secular world. Hence new theologians like Paul M. Van Buren speak of "the secular meaning of the gospel." In his book with that title, Van Buren outlines the historical perspective of the secular Christian who lives his faith in a culture shaped by technology and industrialization. For this man the key to the empirical meaning of the Gospel must be the comparison and relationships between the language about Jesus of Nazareth and certain kinds of experience that we have today. Van Buren insists that "if no family resemblances were allowed between the language of the Gospel and the way in which we speak of being loved by another human being, we should have to abandon all hope of understanding what the Gospel means. But languages do have family resemblances, and it is by noticing them as well as by seeing their limits that we can understand the language of theology. The verification principle shows that theological statements which are meaningless in a secular age when they are taken as straightforward empirical assertions about the world, nevertheless prove to have a use and a meaning as the expressions of a historical perspective with far-reaching empirical consequences in a man's life. In the last analysis, a tree is known by its fruit."[4]

To a large degree Söderblom shared the empirical concerns of the new theologians. The basic difference between them and Söderblom was that he had a breadth of theological vision which stands in marked contrast to the broken and fragmentary character of radical theology in its present stage of development. The vastness and comprehensiveness of that Söderblomian vision saw every empirical fact in relation to the larger context of the whole of reality. No doubt his studies in the history of the world's religions and his many travels had helped to place him in a situation of continuous exposure to the broadest framework of human religions and cultures.

Already in 1897, in an address before the First Congress of the Science of Religion in Stockholm, Söderblom outlined the religious perspective in terms of its empirical consequences for the social well-being and development of the human race. The religious concern for love, justice, and truth was to be translated into concrete, practical social action, even though the religious proprium of the good envisioned by the Gospel would not be completely identical with any social or cultural amount of good achieved by human effort at a certain point in history.

As archbishop, Söderblom put all his influence and power to work for the empirical, tangible realization of the practical concerns of Christianity. But here again he broke through the narrowness of radical theology to the all-embracing, ecumenical perspective of one church, one Lord, one world. All Christians serving a common Lord in a world of human need—that was Söderblom's universal answer to the problem raised by the world and the church in his day. The Stockholm Conference on Life and Work, which marked a milestone in the history of the ecumenical movement and the recovery of the contemporary relevance of Christianity, was largely the work of the ecumenical genius of Archbishop Söderblom. At the same time it was his response to Jesus' call to discipleship and holiness. The saints and holy men of religion were, for Söderblom, those who show by their being and their actions that there is a living God. The lives and works of the true saints are one of the concrete and empirical verifications of the continued action of God in history and human personality.

Thus far we have seen how three motifs of the contemporary radical theology are related to the thought of Nathan Söderblom. The three motifs are: (1) the death of God, (2) obedience to Jesus, and (3) the emphasis on the empirical attitudes of modern man. There still remain three more main themes which pervade the contemporary theological climate and play an important part in the God-is-dead theology at its present stage of evolution. These themes are: (1) the transformation of the traditional form of Christian faith, (2) the problem of suffering, and (3) the affirmation of this world.

The contemporary theological confusion and restlessness has been a matter of great concern to theologians and churchmen everywhere. There are many who ask, Does this period of rapid change signify the coming of the end, the loss of everything that gives specifically religious and Christian meaning and order to human life? Or does the seemingly increasing indifference to the Word of faith which the church proclaims signal the dawn of a great ecumenical future

for the church universal? Some of the new theologians would agree
with Altizer that "there is solace for us in the fact that Israel once
experienced a comparable crisis. Through the catastrophic events of
the Exile, Israel lost everything which was the source of order and
meaning to an ancient people. Banished from their sacred land and
traditions, the exilic Jews were forced to live without their mon-
archy, their shrines and temple, their cultic priesthood. Today we
know that a new form of faith was born out of that crisis. . . . Is
there any reason to believe that our contemporary Christian crisis
is less than that of the ancient Jew in Exile? Just as the Jew was
born out of a passage through the death of his own sacred history,
may we hope that a new Christian will be born out of the death
of Christendom? First, we must recognize that our theology thus
far has only partially responded to Tillich's call for theological contemporaneity. The modern Christian theologian has been not unlike
those postexilic scribes and priests who codified Israel's laws and
traditions, assembled and then gradually canonized a scripture, and
appropriated the prophetic revolution so as to make it the living
foundation of Judaism. In other words, the theologian has for the
most part performed the priestly role of remembering the Christian
past. His function has been one of recollecting the past so as to
relate it to the present. Yet increasingly the theologian has been
forced to play the Proustian role of searching for a lost time, of
desperately attempting to remember a time which has been forgotten, and thus he has been sorely tempted to isolate the Word of
faith from the seemingly faithless reality of our present."[5]

No one worked more diligently than Archbishop Söderblom to
relate the Word of faith to all of reality and history. His thought
provides an overwhelming testimony for the continued revelation
of God. Söderblom argued that it was ridiculous to look upon God's
revelation as finished with the Bible or with Christ. He recognized
that the ultimate source of the kind of theological *malaise* that in our
day has given rise to the God-is-dead "solution" is the loss of any
real sense of the contemporary reality of divine revelation.

If Söderblom were living today, he would probably say that the
radical theology recognizes a real problem of modern man, but the
new theologians of this theological stance try to "solve" the difficulty

by throwing out the baby with the bathwater. His answer to the problem they raise would likely be to refer them to the serious study of contemporary signs of the continuing activity of the living God. In his book on the nature of revelation Söderblom sought to provide criteria for discerning the contemporary signs of a continued divine self-disclosure which is most evident "in three areas of life, in nature, in history and in the moral life. These may be further defined by three phenomena: (1) genius as a phase of nature, (2) the continuity and purposiveness of history, (3) the regeneration of the individual and the formation of character. If this continued revelation takes place within Christendom it marks the continued action of Christ. Belief in and experience of his living power is the identifying characteristic common to all Christianity."[6]

The Christocentric and incarnational approach is characteristic of Söderblom's solution to the problem raised by the transitional situation of theology in the twentieth century. The Word of God became flesh in Jesus of Nazareth and has not stopped being active as a living power in nature, history, and human personality. In the Söderblomian vision Christ, history, nature, and human existence are inseparably related at all times. Furthermore, by reason of the incarnation, the Word of faith is continuous with all of reality and cannot be isolated from the process of reality.

Some of the contemporary representatives of radical theology have insisted that the Christian must be defined as one who has freely chosen Jesus because he is drawn to him and has given him his allegiance. The Christian is distinguished from other men by his obedience to Jesus and his endeavor to be obedient as Jesus was obedient. This choice is not an arbitrary one, but it is a free choice freely made because the Christian finds in Jesus' way with his fellow men, his life, works, words, and death, something that he does not find anywhere else.

If we were to ask Söderblom what this unique attraction of Jesus Christ is, he would say it is the mystery of vicarious suffering. The incarnate Word of God suffers for his fellow men: this is Christianity's positive response to the problem of suffering; more than that, Jesus as suffering Lord is the clue to the meaning of life. In the most profound ideas and longings of religion and philosophy Söderblom was able to discern a marvelous continuity, going back to the earliest records of history, a continuity of the dim perception that the way of God with men and the way of suffering are inseparable one from the other. This age-old perception of divinity became fully revealed in the flesh and blood of Jesus Christ, the Jew from Nazareth. He is the definitive fulfillment and incarnation of the form of divinity.

It is interesting that Söderblom developed, in the face of theological crisis, affirmations rather similar to those which characterize the answers of the God-is-dead theologians of today, though he was able at the same time to do full justice to the reality of God in a universe in process. Some of the new theologians would with William H. Hamilton raise objections to any transcendent concept of God or divinity on the ground that "if there is divinity apart from Jesus, it is a form of divinity that Jesus as suffering Lord corrects, destroys, transforms. In Jesus the Lord we see for the first time what Christian 'divinity' must be taken to be: it is God withdrawing from all claims to power and authority and sovereignty, and consenting to become himself the victim and subject of all that the world can do. . . . Divinity in Jesus is not withdrawal from the world: it is a full consent to abide in the world, and to allow the world to have its way with it."[7]

The ability of Söderblom to find the transcendent in the immanent, and the immanent in the transcendent, offers a valuable corrective to the theological perspective of radical theology. In his book on the history of Christ's Passion, *Kristi pinas historia,* he takes up a concern similar to that of the new theologians, a concern for the reality of the humanity of God, but he does it without losing sight of the reality of God on the one hand, and on the other hand without failing to do justice to the relatedness and continuity of Jesus' form of divinity with the other historical forms of divinity, no matter how primitive, distorted, or degenerate they may be. The universal viewpoint of Söderblom would place the problem of radical theology in the context of the whole of human culture, religion, and philosophy. Among the most important things that the new theologians of our day might learn from Archbishop Söderblom is the insight that there are no isolated meanings, but every true meaning is related to every other meaning in the realm of truth and the process of reality. The God-is-dead theologians, as well as most other contemporary theologians, are caught in the trap of a narrow and limited concern. They need the ecumenical, catholic vision of Söderblom, a vision of the structure of religion as a universal process of interrelated meanings which mutually enrich and enhance one another.

Closely related to the seemingly irretrievable loss of real transcendence is the this-worldly orientation of the new radical theology. Our contemporary world of rapid social change, mass media, automation, and technological innovation is hailed by the new theologians with a feeling of hope and optimism. This optimism is in some ways quite unlike the earlier optimistic belief in inevitable progress, which ignored the powerful presence of evil and was insensitive to the suffering and tragedy of human life. It is also quite unlike the morbid pessimism which marked the earlier part of this century and gave rise to expressions such as T. S. Eliot's *Wasteland* and Picasso's *Guernica*. The new optimism of the God-is-dead theologians is based on the realization that the odds are for a gradual but substantial change in the shape of human life on this earth. The persistent optimism that characterizes American life today, and is quite noticeable in the civil rights movement and its firm belief that "we shall overcome," demands that modern men drop the old hostile attitudes against technology and urbanization, speed and space, and begin to learn to respond positively to the decisive changes in our natural and cultural life.

In his studies of the religions of the world, Söderblom discovered that the valuation and importance of this-worldly pursuits is characteristic of genuinely prophetic religion. In his last great book, *The Living God*, he argues that in Zoroastrianism, as well as in Judaism and Christianity, this world, human labor, and the struggle for social justice are of decisive significance for the religious goals of these religions. This attitude toward the phenomenal world stands in contrast to the other-worldly, metaphysical, and mystical tendencies of Eastern religions like Buddhism and Hinduism. For these religions nature, history, the world, and the activities of human life are *maya*, unreal, illusion. Archbishop Söderblom would agree with the new theologians that past and contemporary history is the crucial sphere where the relevance of religion and its power to change gradually the human situation are tested. But he would go beyond radical theology and its optimistic affirmation of this world to emphasize that history and the human spirit are self-transcendent. They point beyond themselves to what is yet to come and to be revealed.

As a son of the evangelical revival in Sweden toward the end of the nineteenth century, Söderblom tended to express the transcendent element in history and culture in the metaphors and poetic language of revivalism. But he was well aware of the ephemeral effects of revivalism when it is built on emotional straw fires and a one-sided presentation of the essence of Christianity. Consequently, when Söderblom became Archbishop of Uppsala, he organized revival campaigns which aimed at presenting the whole Gospel, that is, Christianity in its historic fullness, in its evangelicity as well as in its catholicity. He would never permit evangelical and catholic Christianity to be isolated from its cultural and historical context. Faith without culture was to him like a fish without water.

As an ardent adept of twentieth-century science, Söderblom always coupled his evangelical and catholic vision with a concern for the scientific examination of religion. Every affirmation of transcendence had to be tested and criticized in the light of scientific principles and methods which had proved their value in the natural life of man in this world. If the religious metaphors of the revival piety permeated Söderblom's positive affirmation of this world, then his respect for and devotion to scientific procedures penetrated his entire perspective on the possibilities of modifying human existence. The enormous this-worldly optimism which was implied in Söderblom's efforts for universal world peace and his organization of the Stockholm Conference on Life and Work, one of the decisive events in the history of the ecumenical movement, indicates a concern for contemporary relevance which is remarkably like that of the new theologians of our day. But unlike the radical theologians of our time he was both more evangelical and catholic *and* more universal in his outlook and assessment of the problem confronting modern man as he encounters the challenge of Jesus the Lord. And unlike much radical theology of the contemporary God-is-dead variety, Söderblom was profoundly aware of, and sensitive to, the depth dimension of man's life in this world.

The archbishop never lost sight of the fact that there are depths and heights of the natural life of man which are more adequately expressed by the metaphors of revelation and the language of religious meanings than by the blind reduction of the sacred to the profane which at many points is insensitive to the real mystery of life and of human suffering, tragedy, joy, and hope. A reduction like this fails to account for, and do justice to, what both religious and secular men know to be true about the human situation and the complicated web and interdependent matrix of human existence. Here again Söderblom urges us to see the natural life of man in the total context of reality and in the perspective of the whole of human history. The history of man on earth provides an overwhelming testimony to the human intuition of the nature and spirit of the divine, an intuition which stretches all the way from the caveman of prehistory to the modern high-rise dweller in a great metropolis.

THE SECULAR CITY

One of the great contemporary challenges to Christianity is how to make sense of the urbanization and secularization of human life and thought in the twentieth century. The symbol of this process, which is transforming human existence, is the secular city. In an effort to understand the secular city from a theological perspective, men like Harvey Cox have argued that we must begin with the recognition that "the rise of urban civilization and the collapse of traditional religion are the two main hallmarks of our era and are closely related movements. Urbanization constitutes a massive change in the way men live together, and became possible in its contemporary form only with the scientific and technological advances which sprang from the wreckage of religious world-views. Secularization, an equally epochal movement, marks a change in the way men grasp and understand their life together, and it occurred only when the cosmopolitan confrontations of city living exposed the relativity of the myths and traditions men once thought were unquestionable."8 Both urbanization and secularization are emergent realities in process, not static facts.

Archbishop Söderblom anticipated a theology of culture and rapid social change as a necessary adaptation in order to enhance the role of Christianity as a vital and relevant force shaping human life and thought in a situation similar to Cox's "technopolitan" environment. Throughout his writings, Archbishop Söderblom sought to understand industrialization, technology, urbanization, and modern politics from a theological point of view. Characteristically, his stance was always ecumenical, aiming at universality and synthesis. This makes him a needed corrective of the atomistic tendencies in much of contemporary theology. He is a trustworthy guide in the search for a universal and ecumenical synthesis. Many contemporary theologians are confused and perplexed by their inability to achieve a truly universal theological synthesis. The theological reflections of Nathan Söderblom contain many profound and helpful suggestions as to how the City of God and the secular city can be most creatively and fruitfully related in the process of history.

Basic to Söderblom's theology of twentieth-century urbanization and technology is his view of the nature of God's action in history. God has not stopped revealing himself in word and deed. His creative activity does not end with the Bible or with Christ, nor is it confined to the biblical field of vision. The reconciling and redemptive action of God is understood, at least dimly, in every religion that has occurred in the process of history. Since we know of no people, however primitive or advanced, that did not have religion, we may speak of a universal recognition of divine power in every human culture. Söderblom places great stress on the historical character of religion and theology. Religion is process, and theology is never an absolute, discontinuous, static entity. Theology is always adapting and changing and decaying: it is continuous with, and related to, historical process.

Modern theology is in a good position to appreciate Söderblom's insight that theology is a historical process shaped by continual adaptation and adoption of meanings and symbols drawn from the continuous movement of historical events. Theology must not be viewed as a body of divine truths cast into holy doctrines which men need only to repeat. There are no absolute ideas or unchangeable meanings in historical process. Söderblom's studies of the Bible, the history of Christian thought, and the history of religions confirmed his basic conviction that theology must always speak to the contingencies of human history and culture if it is to be vital. That theology ought to speak to twentieth-century urban culture is inherent in the evangelical and catholic Word of faith. That theology can speak to modern urban existence becomes evident when we consider the historical character of theology as a continuous and continual process of adoption and adaptation. Theology is continuous with all other realms of reality, and it is continually changing from year to year.

Can theology speak to a historical situation which neither the Bible nor the history of theology could, or did, anticipate? Yes, said Söderblom, yes, in spite of the fact that the old, traditional theology of the church speaks out of a context that knew nothing about, and in fact has often resisted, the modern historical situation of man. If we look at the great saints of the church who have determined the course of Western theology—men like Saint Augustine and Saint Thomas, or for that matter even the Reformers from John Wycliffe to John Wesley—we are struck by the fact that between them and us today in most instances there is more discontinuity than continuity at the level of basic assumptions, ideas, and world views.

Söderblom would undoubtedly warn today's theologians to be very cautious in their adaptation of biblical and traditional Christian views to the secular existence of modern men in urban society. The continuity between the saints of the church and the Christian in today's secular city is a continuity of the spirit, not of the letter. Saints, in Söderblom's view, are men and women who by their being and lives reveal the power of God. Insofar as theology is the *logos* about *theos,* or the language of man about God, theological continuity between the past and the present must be sought in the creative power of the living God, a power which works chiefly through human agency in history. For Söderblom the self-identity and continuity of theology is not a matter of language but of the power of God. Language changes, and the language of one era or people in history is frequently more discontinuous than continuous with that of another period and culture. One culture may use God-language, and another may find such language meaningless. Some primitive religions have felt this way, and so have some of the higher religions. Two and one half millennia ago the Buddha dismissed God-language as meaningless, and today the God-is-dead theologians may do the same for Christianity. From the Söderblomian perspective, there is no reason why God could not reveal his power in the secular city in forms appropriate to the secularity of the modern technopolis. Indeed, the incarnation and the cross should lead Christian theology to suspect just that.

Söderblom's attempt to prove the existence of God through the scientific study of the history of religions on the one hand, and on the other hand through the emergence in history of human religious, artistic, and political genius and the universal human urge to ideals of conduct, has important implications for a theological interpretation of the distinguishing tone and style of the secular city. One of these implications is that theology must find where in the ethos of the secular city the power of God is at work creating, maintaining, reconciling, transforming, judging, and redeeming. At the same time, a theology of secular culture must determine where and what structures, self-seeking persons, and hardened hearts are contradicting and frustrating the gradual realization and fulfillment of all of God's promises.

Present-day theologians of the secular city like Harvey Cox have pointed out that modern technopolitan man does not live as natural man but as secular, urban man. He participates in a quite unnatural, artificial environment. Concrete, steel, and glass have replaced his natural habitat. His food is no longer natural but is chemically pasteurized, preserved, colored, and otherwise treated. His clothes are no longer made of natural but of artificial, synthetic fibers. The environment and the ethos of the secular city are so different from those of natural man that it is quite plausible to argue with Gibson Winter for the emergent reality of "the new creation as metropolis." The contemporary setting of man is the artifact of the secular city. It is man-made, not given by nature. This is not to deny that it could not have been made without given, natural raw materials and resources. But the significant and decisive thing about the new creation as metropolis is that which is made by man, not that which is given. Contemporary urban man lives in an environment of his own creation.

The theological insights of Nathan Söderblom can provide a valuable aid to the Christian understanding of the new, "supernatural" situation of the new humanity of the secular city. One of the basic distinctions in Söderblomian thought is that between natural religion and religion of revelation. Natural religions look to the cosmos, the gods, and metaphysics. When the gods are of no more help to man, mystical self-salvation and metaphysical speculation take over. The value and reality of this world are called into question and denied, and religion becomes psychology. Religions of revelation—which for Söderblom included such nonbiblical religions as Zoroastrianism and Islam, but which in the Western world are most clearly represented by Judaism and Christianity—look to history and human personality as the primary *loci* of the revelation of God. The revelation of God means for Söderblom primarily the power of God manifesting itself in history and human personality. Divine revelation does not refer to the occult communication of infallible, "revealed" truths or absolute dogmas.

From the Söderblomian point of view the quite unnatural, nonmystical, and nonmetaphysical setting of the man of the secular city constitutes a confirmation, rather than a denial, of the basic historical perspective of biblical religion. It is not without reason that the new creation as metropolis has risen in the Judeo-Christian West, and from here is now spreading to every nation on earth. In the secular city, man, not nature, is the threat and the great promise of the present and the future. Here again the thought of Archbishop Söderblom is most relevant and enlightening. He stressed that the central locus of divine power is man as fellow man, history, and human personhood, not the sacred rock or the holy cow. The uniqueness of Christianity is that here the action of God is revealed in human form, and not in rocks or animals or other natural phenomena.

Therefore, if we want to understand secularization and urbanization from a theological perspective, we must look upon the technopolitan setting of urban man as the portent of a new divine grace mediated by history and human persons. The fact that the new creation as metropolis is as yet an unfulfilled promise must not be interpreted as a denial of its promising future. For Söderblom no ethos that places history and human agency in the central focus of responsibility and creativity can be viewed as threatening total alienation from the process of reality. For the type of religion that Söderblom termed "the religion of revelation," *uppenbarelsereligion,* the nearest thing to ultimate reality that man can know, appears in the midst of human history with its partial successes and failures and its joy, tragedy, and hope. The Söderblomian vision urges us therefore to become aware of the kind of historical consciousness that enables us to look at history theologically, and to reflect on the ethos of which we are a part, both in terms of its normative aspects and in terms of its origins and goals.

Theological reflection on the ethos of modern social and cultural developments must be directed toward those pervasive character- istics that can be identified and treated in the context of the tension between positive and negative values in the secular city. This con- text prevents the theological effort from being swallowed up by urban culture on the one hand, and from becoming completely against metropolitan culture on the other. Religion must side with the positive values of social development and against its negative values. The continuing task of religion in the twentieth century—a task that Söderblom outlined in his constructive statement on *Reli- gion and Social Development,* and which provided the theoretical backbone of the practical Christianity of the ecumenical Life and Work movement—is to live in the tension between the positive and negative values of the social development of the secular city, in order to change practically as well as theoretically the hypothetical models by which the ethos of the modern technopolis is analyzed.

Already in 1925, at the Stockholm Conference on Life and Work, Söderblom was calling for something akin to what Cox has termed "a theology of social change." The archbishop's understanding of the rapidly accelerating social development of mankind in the twentieth century made it a matter of great urgency to overcome the static theology which dominated much of the thinking of the Faith and Order movement. At the Faith and Order Conference at Lausanne, in 1927, it almost came to a showdown between the protagonists of the priority of doctrinal agreement as the condition of Christian unity and cooperation, and Archbishop Söderblom's dynamic process theology and his dominant concern for practical Christian relevance in a rapidly changing world.

The relevance of Söderblom for today becomes quite evident when we hear contemporary technopolitan theologians like Cox, who are trying to wake us up to the fact that "we are all trying to live in an age of accelerating change with a static theology. Since the phrase *rapid social change* serves often merely as a euphemism for *revolution,* the issue could be put even more bluntly: we are trying to live in a period of revolution without a theology of revolution. The development of such a theology should be the first item on the theological agenda today."[9] Söderblom was acutely aware of the necessity for a theology of rapid social change. The old, traditional creeds of Christendom do not address themselves to the problems of social development, urbanization, and technology. Therefore an alteration of the old creeds will not get us a theology of social change. Consequently he insisted that "what we need is a new confession of faith. I do not mean any alteration in the old creeds of the Church, but a clear expression of the teaching of Christ and our Christian duty with regard to the brotherhood of nations, to the fundamental moral laws for the shaping of society, and to the activity of Christian love and charity. Just as in the old Church the enunciation of dogmas was preceded by eager discussion and profound investigation, so in our time too the enunciation of the new dogmas that we need to urge us on and guide us, is being prepared by the investigations and reflections of individual Christians and the joint efforts of larger and smaller groups. And just as certain parts of the creeds of old are paradoxical expressions of ideas that Christianity must advocate, but human thought cannot penetrate and systematize, so perhaps Christianity's new confession of faith in a supernatural brotherhood and Christian principles for social and economic life must stop at clearly conceived propositions and sacred tasks without being able to combine them into a logical unity. But our duty is clear. I do not think we can or ought to be contented with anything less."[10]

Söderblom's skepticism about the possibility of developing a clear, logical, and rational theology of rapid social change shows how deeply he himself was involved in the process of social change. As an ecumenical churchman, he understood, however, that unless the new theology of social change gives rise to a new confession of faith, and new Christian social principles which are broad and universal enough to embrace all men and nations, the agricultural as well as the urbanized ones, it will not be adequate in a world in revolution, nor will it be true to the spirit of evangelical and catholic Christianity. He would no doubt criticize the tendency of the "secular city" theologians to overemphasize the urban interests in, and contributions to, a new theology of revolution. The ecumenical vision of Söderblom's "new confession of faith" would see promise in both the metropolis and the small town or rural community. In a new process theology of the new creation as metropolis, there must be hope for the country and the small town, too, if it is to be an adequate theology of social change and development.

NOTES

1. William Hamilton, "American Theology, Radicalism and the Death of God." From *Radical Theology and the Death of God*, copyright © 1966 by Thomas J. J. Altizer and William Hamilton, reprinted by permission of the publishers, The Bobbs-Merrill Company, Inc.
2. Tor Andrae, *Nathan Söderblom* (Uppsala: J. A. Lindblads förlag, 1931), p. 328.
3. Thomas J. J. Altizer, "Creative Negation in Theology." Originally printed in the July 7, 1965, issue of *The Christian Century*. Reprinted in *Frontline Theology* (Richmond, Va.: John Knox Press, 1967). Used by permission.
4. Paul M. Van Buren, *The Secular Meaning of the Gospel* (New York: Macmillan, 1963), p. 199.
5. Altizer, *op cit.*, pp. 864-865.
6. Nathan Söderblom, *The Nature of Revelation*, trans. Frederic E. Pamp (New York: Oxford University Press, 1933), pp. 143-144.
7. William H. Hamilton, *The New Essence of Christianity* (New York: Association Press, 1961), pp. 90-91.
8. Harvey Cox, *The Secular City* (New York: Macmillan, 1965), p. 1.
9. Cox, *op. cit.*, p. 107.
10. Nathan Söderblom, *Christian Fellowship* (New York: Fleming H. Revell Co., 1923), pp. 179-180.

CHAPTER II

THE ECUMENICAL VISION

One of the most significant and universal developments in contemporary Christianity is the ecumenical transformation and reformation of those churches which comprise the vast majority of Christians today. The ecumenical movement is still very young. This means that, on the one hand, all Christians standing inside and outside the movement toward Christian unity have much to learn about ecumenically relevant humility, solidarity, and charity. Much is yet to be done to further the fruitful exchange of those special spiritual and material gifts which each church can contribute to the upbuilding of the living Body of Christ. Despite the triumph of the ecumenical spirit in the World Council of Churches and the Second Vatican Council, there are still many things that stand in the way of a united Christian witness and service in the world. On the other hand, the young ecumenical movement is full of promise. It still has a great future before it as it moves gradually closer to the realization of the coming great church.

As the spirit and practice of ecumenism spread through the churches in ever widening circles, the relevance of Archbishop Söderblom's ecumenical vision becomes more and more apparent. He was an ecumenical world church leader far ahead of his time. Now, and in the crucial years ahead, he can give us invaluable suggestions and guidance for the progress of the ecumenical movement.

THE FIRST STEP: PRACTICAL COOPERATION

One of the guiding principles of Söderblom was pragmatic: Practical Christian cooperation is the most readily available measure for taking first steps in the direction of ecumenical Christian unity.

The history of the ecumenical movement has proved again and again the practical wisdom and almost universal applicability of this Söderblomian principle of ecumenism. In future ecumenical encounters involving Roman Catholic, Protestant, Orthodox Christians, and eventually also those involving Jews and Moslems, the principle will continue to be extremely helpful. Already now there are voices in the World Council of Churches announcing the coming emergence of an "ecumenical perspective on Judaism." Ecumenical theologians like Eugene L. Smith are beginning to realize that "the traditional patterns of Christian evangelism among Jews have suffered from a ludicrous reversal of the situation against which Paul fought in early Jewish Christianity. Paul insisted that a Gentile did not have to become a Jew in order to become a Christian. Today we force a Jew to become a Gentile if he is to become a Christian. A Jew ready to re-think the question of Christ is presented today with the socially abhorrent and theologically gratuitous necessity of deserting his own community and joining a Gentile community if he should come to a confession of Christ's messiahship. Is it impossible to think of a fellowship of Christians, both Jew and Gentile, united in faith and mission? Is it impossible to think of an appeal to Jews within their own community that might mean not just the conversion of individuals, but the infusion of the Jewish community— already so rich in fellowship and achievement—with the riches of Christ? Is it impossible to think that thus God might heal the first great schism within the people of his covenant?

"As Christians, we dare not hope for less. Individual discoveries of the grace of God in Jesus Christ are always reasons for gratitude. However, Israel has a destiny as a people. It is unthinkable that Israel should be absorbed into our divided churches by the multiplication of individual conversions, and lose the historic identity maintained for three millennia. Our aim should be nothing less than that we should be used of God for re-uniting the two separated halves of the people of God."[1]

A practical demonstration of the working out of an ecumenical perspective on Judaism is presently being furnished by the Judeo-Christian mission to high-rise apartment buildings in Chicago's Edgewater community. This program based on cooperation among Prot-

estant, Roman Catholic, and Jew is a unique, probably unprecedented outreach of religious concern. Problems have been encountered in finding financial support, in finding callers, in training
visitors, in interpreting the Judeo-Christian religious visitation program which constitutes the heart of the Edgewater movement, and
in dealing with building managers. They have been resolved ami-
cably and with good will. No individual's faith has been watered
down! Nor has that of any of the seventeen participating churches
and synagogues! Rather the Judeo-Christian congregations are
learning, serving, and doing much practical work in relation to
persons. United in service and mission and religious concern, the
two halves of the people of God are reaching the "cliff dwellers"
with the warmth of human feelings. The spirit of religious faith
and human concern is being released in new and creative ways.
There is no doubt that the spirit of mission, candor, trust, honesty,
cooperation, and ecumenicity is on the march in Edgewater.

The practical principle of Söderblomian ecumenicity will also be
applicable to possible future ecumenical meetings between Christians and Moslems. Islam owes much of its religious inspiration to
Judaism and Christianity. Historians of religion have long recognized
that, together with Judaism and Christianity, Islam belongs to the
three "religions of the book." Today far-sighted thinkers are beginning, under the auspices of the World Council of Churches, to ask
whether the time has not come now for a creative reconsideration
of the question of "Muslims and the finality of Jesus Christ in the
age of universal history." At the present time it is impossible to
predict with certainty what this will lead to. No doubt some will
say that this new spirit in Moslem-Christian relations is just another
illustration of the wisdom of the adage: "If you can't lick 'em, join
'em." But the fact remains that in our time with its ecumenical
spirit, walls of hatred, prejudice, and misunderstanding between
Moslems and Christians are beginning to crumble. In view of this,
men like Daud Rahbar are beginning to ask and to answer the question: "What then is the task before the Church in relation to the
Muslim world?

"First of all Christian scholarship can help in the initiation of
Muslim scholars in the modern discipline of the study of universal

history as a unity, and thus in effective liberation of Muslim scholarship from the histories of the surrounding communities. Over and above the scientific and pragmatist writings about the tradition of Islam, Christian men of *belles lettres* must begin a literary movement that will emancipate educated Christians from their provincialism. A great deal depends on the sensitivity of Christian communication on all levels: in broadcasting, journalism, academics, fiction, plays and poetry . . . . Insensitive polemics and apologetics do more harm than good. The hope of winning Muslims to sympathy with the Christian faith by means of crude criticism of the social shortcomings of Muslim society is a wild one. All societies, including the Christians, are more apt to self-examination today than at any time in the past . . . . Christians should therefore devote themselves in the first place to being truly exemplary, which means having genuine regard and affection for men of all races and creeds."[2]

Söderblom would no doubt rejoice that also the Roman Catholic Church has accepted his basic ecumenical principle according to which cooperation in social and moral concerns is a necessary first step on the road to fuller understanding and unity between representatives of different religions and faiths. This holds true to some degree also of the *Declaration on the Relation of the Church to Non-Christian Religions* promulgated by Vatican II. In section three of the *Declaration* it is stated that the Roman Catholic Church "regards with esteem also the Moslems. They adore the one God, living and subsisting in Himself, merciful and all-powerful, the Creator of heaven and earth, who has spoken to men; they take pains to submit wholeheartedly to even His inscrutable decrees, just as Abraham, with whom the faith of Islam takes pleasure in linking itself, submitted to God. Though they do not acknowledge Jesus as God, they revere Him as a prophet. They also honor Mary, His virgin mother; at times they even call on her with devotion. In addition, they await the day of judgment when God will render their deserts to all those who have been raised up from the dead. Finally, they value the moral life and worship God especially through prayer, almsgiving and fasting.

"Since in the course of centuries not a few quarrels and hostilities have arisen between Christians and Moslems, this sacred synod urges all to forget the past and to work sincerely for mutual understanding and to preserve as well as to promote together for the benefit of all mankind social justice and moral welfare, as well as peace and freedom."[3]

It is indicative of the far-sightedness and continuing relevance of Söderblom's ecumenical vision that these last words of the Vatican *Declaration* on Islam are an almost exact reproduction of parts of Söderblom's platform for the ecumenical Life and Work conference. This does not mean that the Vatican Council Fathers copied him; it simply shows that the ecumenical spirit of Söderblom was far ahead of his time, and that he is worth knowing about today. It is only now that we are beginning to realize the ecumenical implications of what he said back then in the 1920's, and what he did to demonstrate and to realize the fullness of his universal plan for Christian unity. Many devoted ecumenists today are not yet ready for Söderblom's insight that no religion is a product of culture, but that all religion depends on a revelation of the living God. This will come in the years ahead as the spirit of ecumenism continues to open new vistas and brings repentance to many hardened hearts.

RENEWAL, SUPERNATIONALISM, ORGANIZED FORM

Besides the ecumenical principle of the trailblazing significance of practical Christian cooperation, a second Söderblomian principle of Christian unity is that there can be no ecumenicity worthy of the name which does not involve a renewal of the whole church. The continued relevance of this view has been confirmed not only by many leaders of the World Council of Churches, but also by the Roman Catholic *Decree on Ecumenism* promulgated at the Second Vatican Council. Söderblom himself put it to work in the Church of Sweden, which experienced a remarkable revival while he was Archbishop of Uppsala.

A third principle of Söderblom's ecumenism was that the unity of the church must transcend the barriers of nations and races. Ecumenicity cannot and must not submit to the sins of chauvinism and racism. Just how relevant and necessary this principle is can be seen from a report on the closing days of the Second Vatican

Council, when five prelates from the United States, in an unfortunate and inglorious display of chauvinism, joined six bishops from other countries in opposing the statement in the schema on the church in the modern world that "the arms race is an utterly treacherous trap for humanity and one which ensnares the poor to an intolerable degree."[4] The relevance of Söderblom's interracial ecumenical vision is also continually confirmed by the courageous and creative involvement of ecumenical Christians and Jews in the U.S. civil rights movement, and in the continuing concern of the World Council of Churches over racist policies in parts of Africa.

A fourth principle of Söderblom's ecumenical framework was the continued necessity of making visible the Christian unity of the churches in a concrete and living form, especially during the early and formative stages of the ecumenical movement. This principle has been overwhelmingly validated by the ecumenical assemblies of Amsterdam, in 1948, Evanston, in 1954, and New Delhi, in 1961, as well as in the sessions of the Second Vatican Council. Its continued relevance will become even more apparent in the years ahead.

Archbishop Söderblom himself was the leading power behind the ecumenical Life and Work Conference of 1925. This meeting was the first of the large ecumenical meetings of the churches. It made the archbishop's palace in Uppsala the first true ecumenical center of the twentieth century, thanks to his extraordinary courage and ecumenical vision. At this center he brought together churchmen and religious leaders from all over the world at a time when ecumenism in any form still seemed quite unrealistic, and when the churches were still under the influence of the political passions aroused by World War I.

The unifying principle of Söderblom's understanding of ecumenicity was his loyalty and devotion to the church. His evangelical and catholic understanding of Christian unity was that of a committed ecumenical churchman who had matured during the hardships and heartbreaks of the First World War. His pragmatic Christian ecumenism made it natural for him to accept the churches as they were without trying to reconcile or adjust their creeds or their different conceptions of the ministry. The great ecumenical archbishop was driven on by faith in the church catholic to devote the best years of his life to bring the churches to the point when they would reach beyond the walls and barriers of nations, classes, and races, and unite their members in one ecumenical unity.

Söderblom realized that unless he could demonstrate before the eyes of all churches, and indeed before the whole world, the scope of Christian unity in a concrete and living form, the ecumenical movement would never get off the ground. Therefore he was determined to achieve this in the Stockholm Conference on Life and Work. It was not easy, there were many setbacks and disappointments, and much resistance had to be overcome in quarters which viewed the whole ecumenical project as a wild dream and an unsound plan. But the international ecumenical genius of Söderblom triumphed in the end, due in part to the good help of the World Alliance for Promoting International Friendship, the U.S. Church Peace Union, and numerous friends and helpers that he gathered about him partly through his international connections and partly through contacts in Sweden.

Söderblom's ecumenical efforts encountered misunderstanding and opposition in western Sweden, Finland, and Germany. But his unfailing courage, vitality, and humor, and his unwavering loyalty to and faith in the great cause of Christian unity prevailed and made the Stockholm Conference a reality. Well aware of the process character of genuine ecumenicity, he emphasized that this first great ecumenical gathering in the twentieth century was just the beginning of the ecumenical reformation of the churches. Thanks largely to the influence of Söderblom, the word "ecumenical" obtained a permanent place in the contemporary movement toward Christian unity.

The Stockholm Conference, and its continuation, the Universal Christian Council for Life and Work, gave the first great ecumenical impetus to the World Council of Churches, which today represents the most significant, permanent, official instrument and institution of cooperation between churches. These churches are on the march to a great ecumenical future—a future which is unthinkable apart from the legacy of Archbishop Söderblom, and the continued application of those principles and methods of Christian unity which he developed during the formative period of the contemporary movement of ecumenism.

ECUMENICITY AND WORLD PEACE

One of the most urgent contemporary issues is world peace. Söderblom's work for world peace was an integral part of his ecumenical concern, thus expressing a principle of the practice of ecumenism which is becoming increasingly relevant also in the Roman Catholic world—witness Pope John XXIII and his encyclical *Pacem in terris* (Peace on Earth) and the passionate plea for world peace made by Pope Paul VI at the United Nations in New York in 1965. The ecumenical concern for universal peace has been bequeathed by Söderblom as a heritage of the World Council of Churches. The continuing work of the World Council for peace, which is constantly being carried on through its various agencies and commissions, such as the Commission of the Churches on International Affairs (CCIA), gives eloquent testimony to the great value and vitality of this heritage.

The principles of Söderblom's ecumenical quest for universal peace should be known by modern men, because in these principles Söderblom gives conscious and explicit expression to the as-yet unconscious and groping aims and aspirations of the ecumenical movement. A first principle of peace is bound up with the revelation of the living God in history. Söderblom considered his efforts for peace as nothing less than the struggle to recognize the revelation of God as a living reality and process in our world. All the churches are called to work for peace as a sign of obedience to the revelation of God in Christ. In the opening sentence of his lecture on *The Church and Peace,* Söderblom stressed that "peace of heart and peace on earth: These things are urgent for the Church as long as she calls herself by the name of the Prince of Peace."

A second principle of ecumenical peace follows from the mutual interdependence of peace of heart and peace on earth. Peace in the hearts of men has important consequences for their behavior and attitudes in the world, and thus bears directly on the esteem in which they hold the ideal of universal peace. Söderblom considered it a principle of ecumenism that renewal and the promotion of peace must go hand in hand. No universal, ecumenical peace can be had without inner conversion. The utopian's monistic dream of universal peace is unrealistic, because it tends to ignore the fact that there is no practical way to peace other than the narrow and hard way of struggle against hatred, divisiveness, and injustice. Thus, paradoxically, struggle is needed to win peace. It is a struggle against the old Adam in us, with his sins and evil lusts. The nature of the process of historical and personal reality is such that we must face this struggle if we want to be realistic about the possibilities of ecumenical peace. Just as there can be no ecumenism worthy of the name without renewal, so also there can be no ecumenical, universal peace without inner conversion.

A third principle of Söderblom's ecumenical understanding of peace relates the realization of world peace to the establishment of Christian unity. The church's witness for peace, whether made by the Pope, or by Archbishop Söderblom, or by the World Council of Churches, is worth little unless the church itself ceases to be full of strife, divisiveness, and quarrels. "Which is the Church," Söderblom asked, "that can with Christ's own authority proclaim peace through confidence and law and truth? The answer must be: Not a divided Church, full of quarrels and strife, but a reunited Church."[5] Söderblom was well aware that "salt and pepper, acidity and wit have their place also in the internal, spiritual struggles of the Church. But these discussions of the truth should be marked by solidarity with the Master and solidarity with fellow Christians. In accordance with the high-priestly prayer in the seventeenth chapter of St. John the Church must be so united, even outwardly, that the world may see that Christ was sent by the Father. As long as the Church is unable to advance as one man with the message and spirit of the same Master, her task of promoting peace in the world is hampered. Division is of the devil. Unity is of God. Not a false, superficial unity, but a unity in truth."[6]

It is not only desirable, but today it is even necessary for the survival of the human race, that the church should be united as one, great, ecumenical church, filled with the Spirit of the Prince of Peace. The greatest and mightiest champion of universal peace on earth would be a truly ecumenical and united church. The almost continual progress of war in Africa, Asia, and other parts of the world makes the ecumenical witness for peace a most urgent and timely one. The arms race, the spread of nuclear weapons, and the development of missiles in our time are concrete signs of the continuing threat of war which clouds the present and future of the human race.

Söderblom's ecumenical witness for peace is thus an important, urgent, and much needed one, not only because of the present world situation, but also because of the intimate connection between world peace and the cause of Christian unity. This cause represents what is without doubt the most significant and universal development in the church since the Reformation. In view of the reforms promoted by the ecumenical spirit of Vatican II, it is no exaggeration to speak of the ecumenical movement as the continuation of the reformation of the whole Christian church, which was begun at the time of the Reformation. Then the result of reform was the proliferation of sects and churches, disunity, strife, war, dissension, inquisitions, hatred, and misunderstanding. Today the result of ecumenical reform is a tendency toward *aggiornamento*, renewal, ecumenicity, Christian unity, understanding, love of the brethren, and peace. Both, the Protestant Reformation of the past and the ecumenical reformation of the present, are phases of one great historical process aiming at the reform and renewal of the one church of the one Lord.

REVOLUTIONARY REDEFINITION OF CHRISTIAN MISSIONS

A revolutionary redefinition of Christian mission has become a necessity in our time. We are living in a world which is in revolution and in process in an unprecedented manner. Archbishop Söderblom's ecumenical concept of mission pointed to the need for a theology of revolution and process which would help us to rethink and reevaluate the old, traditional concept of missions in a manner congruous with the demands and opportunities of the contemporary world revolution.

This evaluation must lead us to adopt a more flexible and appreciative attitude toward non-Christian religions and cultures. In his epoch-making essay on *The Nature of Revelation*, first published in 1903, Söderblom set it down as a basic principle of understanding the religious and spiritual growth of mankind that "no prophet, no revelation, ever comes before the fulness of time, or until the necessary conditions are at hand (Mark 1:15; Gal. 4:4). These conditions are of historical and psychological nature. They are such that they exclude entirely the conception of divine arbitrariness. No hiatus, no leap takes place. The psychological and historical continuity is unbroken."[7]

THE QUESTION OF POLYGAMY

The relevance of Söderblom's attitude toward non-Christian cultures in the contemporary confusion on the mission fields can be seen everywhere. For instance, one of the problems inhibiting Christian missionary efforts in Africa today is the inability to find a creative, ecumenical, Christian answer to the question of polygamy. At the present time more and more Africans are seeking affiliation with either Christianity or Islam. They do not want to be called pagans and be considered people without culture. But the church's legalistic attitude toward polygamy is frustrating its missionary outreach on the African continent. Failure to come up with an ecumenical policy regarding polygamous households will mean retreat before the great challenge and opportunity to convert the remaining sixty million animists in Africa. And where Christianity retreats or is defeated in Africa, Islam takes over, and what Islam once has, it never surrenders again through conversions. The conversion rate of adult African Moslems to Christianity is negligible. Söderblom's recognition of the historical and psychological continuity of social structures, to which Christianity is brought, can be of great assistance in finding a creative and relevant answer to the question of polygamy.

In equatorial Africa, where polygamy is most prevalent, the infant death rate is more than twenty times that of the United States, and the life expectancy of the African male is only about one-half that of the American male. Under these circumstances polygamy is a law of nature, and not to practice it would mean the extinction of the family, the tribe, or the nation. Economic factors are also involved. For example, the period of lactation lasts from two to three years in certain parts of Africa because the mother is often the only or at least the cheapest source of food for the infant. Many families are so poor that even if other food supplies were available, they could not afford it. Added to the prolonged period of lactation is a widespread, strict taboo against a father's having any sexual contact with his wife during this period. It is likely that these reasons for polygamy will soon be rendered obsolete by the introduction of antibiotics and adequate medical care to reduce the death rate, or of economic measures to enhance the food supply.

There was a time when wives engaged in tilling small farms and in small trading, and thus represented a considerable economic asset. Today this is rapidly becoming a thing of the past as urbanization and mechanization are eroding the wife's economic worth to her husband. A related contemporary phenomenon in Africa is the constant increase in the asking price for brides which will tend to hasten even more the eventual extinction of polygamy. There is another factor involved in polygamy, the factor of prestige. The influence of a tribal chief would soon disappear if he were to be limited to one wife, because his importance is measured by his possessions. A tribal chief may have twenty or thirty wives, many of whom he has inherited from his father and who are old enough to be his grandmothers. In rural Africa where there is no life insurance, the relationship of a man to his inherited wives is essentially that of a guardian to a ward, and has nothing to do with carnal lust. Among the assets and liabilities that a son inherits from his father are his widowed foster mothers for whom he must provide. In Africa the stigma attached to being unmarried is acute, and thus the son, by elevating his inherited widowed foster mothers to the status of wives, removes this stigma.

As the result of a widespread ignorance of the sociological realities of Africa, Söderblom's recognition that in the conditions for the reception of divine revelation there is no place for a hiatus or leap in the unbroken historical continuity of human existence, if not put to creative use in meeting the challenges of contemporary mission work. Foreign mission boards sitting in Europe or America, where serial polygamy has become an accepted and common practice, violate the principle of continuity with their misguided, puritanical, and ignorant zeal for absolute monogamy. Consequently, the policy of Christian missions contradicts the historical process and realities that obtain in Africa. As a result there is nothing more chaotic and morally arbitrary than the attitude of most churches to the question of polygamy and African polygamists. The attitude toward polygamists varies from denomination to denomination and often within the same denomination. Some refuse baptism to polygamists, others openly accept the practice of polygamy among their members. Under these conditions thousands of pagan Africans who wish to join the church are either rebuffed completely, or are denied admittance to the service of Holy Communion. In some African congregations more than ninety percent of the total membership is thus barred from the rights and privileges of church membership, because the responsible father refuses to break up his home, to abandon to possible prostitution wives whom he loves and has married in good faith, and to deprive his children of the love of their own father. The urgent need for a Söderblomian perspective on Christian missions is nowhere more evident than in equatorial Africa today.

REVELATION FOR REVOLUTION

One of the most pervasive of Söderblom's convictions was that the process character of reality makes it impossible to take the old, traditional theologies and methods and simply apply them to the present. Both revelation and reality are essentially process, characterized by continual change, continuous development, and advancing enrichment both in terms of meaning and in terms of increasing complexity. In our time of rapid social change the old is passing away quickly and the new is still obscure. Because of the relational character of historical process, in the space age, revolutionary events in one area will almost immediately affect all other areas of life.

The old foundations are shaken or crumbling, and it is continually uncertain what will remain. Events with revolutionary effects on almost every sphere of life are taking place with bewildering rapidity. That which Söderblom called the "dualism" of history and personal reality is evident in the strange paradox of, on the one hand, a rising optimism and hopeful expectation among the great mass of mankind, and of the equally common uncertainty, fear, confusion, and despair, on the other hand. On the one side, the contemporary world is presented with unprecedented opportunities for the advancement and enhancement of human life; on the other side, the threat of total annihilation of human life, culture, and religion hangs over the world like the sword of Damocles.

Archbishop Söderblom understood the rapid social, technological, and spiritual changes of our time, including the ecumenical movement, as both the pressure of the world in process and the continued action and revelation of God. The living God is at work in the process of world revolution today. Söderblom sought to determine how Christians may be led to a renewed vision and ecumenical awareness of God's continuing activity in historical process. From the archbishop's point of view the fact that the traditional patterns of missions used in the past century are outmoded, and already today are no longer followed in many places, need not mean that the forces of the Antichrist have gained the upper hand. This development must rather be viewed as a historical transformation of traditional missionary concepts which forces Christians in every nation on earth to reconsider the calling of the church in today's world.

An example of the relevance of Söderblom's process view of missions is furnished by the present missionary exodus from the traditional Japanese mission fields. The reason for this exodus is the fact that there is no adequate place for Christian workers from abroad in Japanese organizations like the Kyodan, the United Church of Christ in Japan, which have a surplus of ordained clergy. Young and eager missionaries from abroad are frustrated in their attempts to integrate their efforts into the structure of the Japanese church. The chief problem in the use of foreign missionaries in Japan today is to find for them opportunities commensurate with their interest and abilities. In church structures that already are overcrowded with a surplus of native clergy, these opportunities must be sought outside the traditional structural setup of the church and not within this structure. Söderblom continually stressed that missions must be changing, be in process, and spearhead the church's creative advance into novel ways of serving Christ through the church. Creativity and imagination are needed desperately in the churches of Japan and America in order to find new opportunities for missionaries from abroad.

The total Christian membership in Japan—Roman Catholic, Protestant, and Orthodox combined—is less than one percent of the population. The conversion rate to Christianity is below the annual population increase. Yet there is a surplus of indigenous Japanese clergy in some denominations, and new, eager missionaries from overseas are frustrated in their attempts to conform to the requirement that the foreign missionary must be under the ecclesiastical jurisdiction as well as under the spiritual guidance of the Japanese churches. Söderblom's spirit of creativity and change in missions at home and abroad is most relevant in this situation. The primary need of the Christian missionary endeavor in contemporary Japan is not to produce more clergy, but to be flexible, creative, and bold in its outreach to a culture which offers almost unlimited opportunities to Christian missionary endeavors. In Japan one finds an openness and eagerness to relate to foreigners—if they have sympathetic appreciation of Japanese culture and history—an openness which is unsurpassed in most other mission fields. Japan's culture is in process, it is a rich and creatively developing culture with a remarkable openness to rapid social change and, at many points, to influences from overseas. In this situation missionaries need freedom and unstructured time to explore new possibilities for creative witness and service outside the old, traditional structures of the Japanese churches and foreign missions.

In reconsidering Christian missionary strategy in the contemporary world, it must be kept in mind that the last great missionary expansion during the nineteenth and early twentieth centuries coincided with the economic, political, and cultural spread of the West into all parts of the world. Today this expansion has largely been halted or reversed. Consequently, Christian missionaries can no longer advance with the dominant and expanding political and cultural forces. Rather, Christianity must now learn again to advance against the stream.

THE CHANGED MISSION SITUATION

Basically there are three related reasons for the contemporary transformation of the missionary situation. First, there is the challenge of a growing nationalism. The traditional mission fields are becoming emerging nations proud of their own cultural and historical traditions. Western cultural imperialism is being rejected. Söderblom's sensitive appreciation of the historical concreteness of historic cultures and religions can be a valuable guide here. From his studies in the history of religions he had learned that historical forms of religion and culture cannot be reduced to a common denominator without violating the integrity of historical structures and destroying their life force. Several important guidelines for missions follow from this.

(1) Christian missions must not be a cultural export. For instance, European and American church architecture is fine for the West, but in the equatorial mission fields of Africa, Indonesia, and Latin America this type of architecture looks more often than not like a symbol of Western culture imposed on, and transposed to, an area of the world that has its own unique, beautiful, symbolical, and functional architectural tradition. Native Christians around the equator have their own culture and want to make use of it so that as Christians they can have one more way of identifying themselves with their nation and people.

(2) The traditional work of missionaries must be taken over by indigenous Christian leadership. The training of national clergy and laymen to continue the work begun by Western missionaries is one of the most urgent requirements in the mission enterprise of the church today.

(3) The peculiar situation of the younger churches in predominantly non-Christian nations demands an increased emphasis on a nonprofessional ministry. The key to the future of Christianity in the traditional mission fields will be lay teachers and evangelists, men and women who will be working in secular jobs. They must be trained without being taken away from their jobs while preparing for the nonprofessional ministry.

(4) The special condition of each of the emerging new nations should be respected by Christian missions. Support should not be cut off from missions if they merge with other Christian groups in order to make a more effective witness for Christ under the difficult circumstances which surround the Christian minority in their country. In the countries of the younger churches the predominantly non-

Christian society is very skeptical of the testimony brought by Christians who refuse to have anything to do with their fellow Christians who are working right next to them in the same area. Söderblom recognized clearly that the ecumenical approach is a must, not only for the Christian churches of the West, but especially also for the younger churches. He himself had come to the ecumenical movement through the Student Missionary Movement, and he realized that great missionary councils had been formative in the history of twentieth-century ecumenism.

A second reason for the contemporary transformation of the missionary situation has been the resurgence of non-Christian religions. For instance, the union of rising nationalism and Islamic self-consciousness has revitalized Moslems in Africa and Asia. And Hinduism, united with a recovery of Indian cultural self-consciousness, has become confident that it has an ocean of truth and insight which can absorb whatever other religions may pour into it without losing its identity, truth value, and religious power.

A third reason for reconsidering Christian missions in a world in rapid change is the spread of Western science and technology in such a way that a universal tendency toward one world civilization is already discernible. The contemporary formation of a single world culture dominated by science and technology includes a complete framework of thought and practice permeated by the belief that man himself can master history and control nature, and thus use his power to create a better future for himself and his children. In this framework there is at present little or no place for any of the traditional God concepts of mankind.

The response to the challenges presented by scientism, the revival of non-Christian religions, and nationalism must be, according to Söderblom, constituted by a movement away from the type of missionizing that tied Christianity to a particular nation or culture. The renewal of missions which has become unavoidable now must be centered around a creative rediscovery and reaffirmation of Jesus Christ as the one, common Master of all missionaries. No longer Caesar, or the foreign mission board, or the enlightenment of Western culture, but the cross must be the central message of contemporary missionary witness. In his reflections on *Christian Missions and Na-*

tional Politics Söderblom stressed that "missions and missionaries should be regarded and treated as being first and foremost servants not of politics or temporal authority but of Christ. Any other principle could only mean death and corruption for missions."[8]

For the evangelical catholic Söderblom, to be a servant of Christ and to serve the cause of ecumenicity was one and the same thing. The belief in, and devotion to, the one Lord Jesus Christ and the one holy catholic and apostolic church is an inseparable part of the ecumenical creed of the church. The relevance of Söderblom's emphasis on the ecumenical nature of contemporary missions is illustrated by Christian missionary endeavors in Latin America. The population explosion and the great number of irreligious and faithless people in that part of the hemisphere make it urgent and necessary that Protestants and Roman Catholics work together there without fear, suspicion, or senseless and malicious competition.

Fortunately it is only the Mormons, Jehovah's Witnesses, and other "evangelical" groups that engage in distasteful street preaching and the distribution of crude anti-Roman Catholic propaganda in Latin America. The great Protestant churches, like the Lutheran, Episcopal, Presbyterian, Methodist, and Baptist, realize the need for an ecumenical witness together with, and not against, the Roman Catholic Church, which until the last century was for all practical purposes the one and only Christian church for Latin Americans. Since the beginning of the twentieth century Protestants have multiplied more than one hundredfold, and now number more than ten million. There can be little doubt that Protestant success in Latin America challenges and upgrades the work of the Roman Catholic Church there. At the same time, Latin American Protestantism will be encouraged to produce a more faithful and thorough Christian witness. If all churches and denominations—Protestant, Orthodox, and Roman Catholic alike—renounce all bigotry, suspicion, and wasteful duplication of effort, their simultaneous ministries will be good not only for the three main branches of Christendom, but also for the people of Latin America. That the spirit of good will and ecumenism should rule in Latin America is all the more necessary in view of the fact that even the best and the most that Roman Catholics, Orthodox, and Protestants can do for Christ and his church in that part of the world will not be good enough nor sufficient to meet the spiritual, moral, and socio-economic needs of the present generation or of the generation to come.

The response of Christianity to the challenge of the contemporary world revolution must be a thoroughgoing ecumenism at home and abroad, in missions as well as in established Christian strongholds. Söderblom viewed this kind of ecumenism both as a genuinely biblical recovery of Christ's will for his church and as a necessary and long overdue response of radical renewal. In one of his lectures he raised the question whether the turmoil and rapid social and cultural transformation of the contemporary world and church was the sign that we are moving toward a new religious renewal. His answer was that we will see a renewal of the church only as we regain with new clarity and devotion the essential vision of genuine Christianity, the ecumenical vision of a world-wide church united around the central symbol of Christian faith, the sign of the mystery of the cross. The church must be renewed by the Spirit of God, the Spirit of ecumenical unity and vicariously suffering love. The church can regain the power to proclaim the Word of God in terms relevant to our time only by a radical ecumenical renewal of its own life. Today the church and its missionary outreach need more than anything else an inner revolution commensurate with the process of world revolution in which the whole of mankind is presently involved. To this world in process and in rapid social change, the prophetic and universal ecumenical vision of Archbishop Söderblom addresses itself with unique clarity and relevance. Among the modern Christian revolutionaries of the twentieth century, he stands out as a dynamic prophet of Christian unity and renewal.

NOTES

1. Eugene L. Smith, "Ecumenical Perspective on Judaism," *The Ecumenical Review* XVII (October, 1965), 355.
2. Daud Rahbar, "Muslims and the Finality of Jesus Christ in the Age of Universal History," *The Ecumenical Review* XVII (Oct., '65), 367-368.
3. Second Vatican Council, *Declaration of the Relation of the Church to Non-Christian Religions* (Huntington, Indiana: Our Sunday Visitor, 1965), p. 5a.

4. "Placet, An Editorial Appraisal of Vatican II," *The Christian Century,* LXXXII, No. 51 (December 22, 1965), p. 1563a.

5. Nathan Söderblom, *The Church and Peace* (Oxford: Oxford University Press, 1929), p. 28.

6. *Ibid.,* p. 29.

7. Söderblom, *The Nature of Revelation,* p. 33.

8. Nathan Söderblom, "Christian Missions and National Politics," *International Review of Missions* VIII (January-October, 1919), 497.

CHAPTER III

SÖDERBLOM'S LIFE AND THOUGHT

The preceding two chapters have dealt with the contemporary significance of Archbishop Nathan Söderblom. Having thus set the stage for a more thorough inquiry into the fascinating life and thought of this great ecumenical church father of the twentieth century, we are now ready to proceed to a concise biographical introduction. This will help the reader to understand Söderblom in the context of his own time and to place his major works and lasting contributions in their proper historical perspective.

CHILDHOOD

Nathan Söderblom was born on January 15, 1866, at Trönö in the Swedish province of Hälsingland. The gentle and persuasive piety of his mother made her Söderblom's first teacher of religion. His father was a Swedish Lutheran pastor *(kyrkoherde)* with a deep, fiery, genuine piety. The passionate, untrammeled religious piety of Nathan's father Jonas made a lasting and decisive impression on Nathan Söderblom's understanding of the essence of religion, revelation, the church, and the Christian life. He grew up as one of the greatest sons of the evangelical revival of nineteenth-century Sweden, and a pietistic strand remained with him throughout his entire lifetime. Swedish pietism helped him to develop a keen sense for the genuinely religious, which later enabled him to discern elements of genuine religion in non-Christian religions. The sensitivity for the specifically religious, as distinct from the moral, also formed the basis of his criticism of Albrecht Ritschl, his admired teacher. He felt Ritschl lacked that untamed, passionate religious instinct which pervaded the writings of Luther and the spirit of Swedish pietism.

The sermons of Jonas Söderblom consisted chiefly of biblical passages and quotes from Luther's writings. Nathan Söderblom's biographer, Tor Andrae, reports that Jonas was able to reproduce up to twenty minutes of continuous quotes from the works of Luther. Nathan shared his father's love of Luther, a love which was broadened, deepened, and enlightened by Nathan's study of Ritschl, who did much to help him cross the chasm between the pious country parish and the almost anti-Christian atmosphere at the University of Uppsala without losing his love of the great hero of the Protestant Reformation. In Söderblom's concept of revelation the powerful personality of Luther occupied a prominent place as one of the greatest religious geniuses of all time—and genius, for Söderblom, was one of the portals of divine revelation.

Jonas Söderblom stimulated his son Nathan to learn to play piano, organ, and the French horn. Nathan Söderblom's musical sensitivities were particularly tuned to the role of music in the continuous proclamation of the revelation of God in the church. Later in his life he spoke of some of the great works of Bach, especially his Passion music, as a "fifth gospel," because of his conviction that this music penetrated into the very essence of the Gospel.

STUDENT DAYS

In the fall of 1883, Nathan Söderblom enrolled as a candidate for the ministry at the University of Uppsala, Sweden. There he became a member of the student missionary group which became an organized society in the spring of 1884. This membership was of great significance for his later life and thought, because the student missionary movement became the training ground for many of the leading figures of the ecumenical movement in the twentieth century. Also, the student missionary group continued the missionary interest which was so prominent in his father, and moved it to a higher, more informed and universal sphere, yet without loss of the genuinely biblical and Lutheran pietistic emphasis.

Two emphases of the student missionary society were of particularly important influence on Nathan Söderblom. One was the international, universal spirit of missions, with its desire to know other peoples and languages in order to be able to communicate with them. The other was the serious, scientific interest which characterized the meetings of the student missionary movement at Uppsala University. They met not only to be edified but also to engage in the scientific study of missions, history, and the history of religions. Söderblom received here his first taste of the history of religions, which later was to assume so prominent a role in his theological, historical, psychological, and devotional writings.

His ecumenical vision also received its first stimulation here in the student missionary movement. As representative of the Uppsala chapter of the missionary society he took part in the Christian Student Conference of 1890 at Dwight L. Moody's summer home in Northfield, Massachusetts. There he made the acquaintance of John R. Mott, the Frenchman Wilfred Monod, and other leading figures in the early phase of the ecumenical movement. Deeply impressed by the ecumenical spirit of the gathering he vowed to devote his life to the cause of Christian unity.

In the first volume of the Uppsala student missionary news magazine, of which Söderblom was the editor for four years, we have the earliest document of the writings of Söderblom, a lecture about St. Ansgar, bishop of Hamburg and Bremen and apostle to Denmark and Sweden. In this lecture, entitled "Sweden's First Christian Teacher," he asked whether St. Ansgar, notwithstanding his ascetic piety, was really a great man, that is, a man of originality, genius, and decisive action. This question was typical of Söderblom, for whom saints were men and women of religious, political, or artistic genius whose lives were a living proof that God was continually active and revealing himself.

Söderblom's view of revelation through prophetic genius clarified for him the nature of the authority of the Bible. The significance of the Scriptures was for him grounded in the fact that the Holy Scriptures are a personal, living, historical testimony of people who have lived under the power of the living God, who have seen his mighty acts and have heard his voice. Divine revelation is mediated by creative personalities and the work of genius in history, rather than primarily by a book of divine oracles or a textbook of dogmatic propositions. In the attempt to understand the personal testimony

of the Bible, religion and science must work together. Historical research, literary criticism, and scientific discoveries appear to stand
in irreconcilable conflict with biblical revelation only as long as we
fail to recognize that God reveals himself in historical process, not
in supernatural oracles or arbitrary interventions in the process of
reality. The quest of faith for the living God, and the scientific
search for the continuity and meaning of nature and history must
in the Söderblomian viewpoint mutually enhance, support, and en-
courage one another.

Söderblom's creative answer to the problem of the relationship
between science and religion effected a spiritual liberation in many
of his contemporaries. His view of the essence of reality and meaning as being a continuous process of personal and historical relationships helped to bring out more clearly the essential relatedness
of religion and science. There is reason to believe that the process
theology of Archbishop Söderblom will become increasingly relevant
as theology moves away from static forms and toward a theology
of revolution which replaces the concept of substance with that of
process. Contemporary theologians of Protestantism like Harvey
Cox have emphasized the need for "a theology of rapid social
change." In the Roman Catholic world the evolutionary process
theology of the late Father Pierre Teilhard de Chardin is heralding
the dawn of a new era of theological creativity. Roman Catholic
theologians and philosophers are cautiously beginning to recognize
that his theology of procession offers a new alternative to the old,
traditional Thomistic theology of substance. A number of theologians
have been attracted by the philosophy of organism developed by
Alfred North Whitehead, who made process the basic and pervasive
characteristic of reality. The signs are mutiplying that Söderblom's
influence will continue to grow.

In 1893 Nathan Söderblom was ordained and was assigned the
position of chaplain to the mental hospital of Uppsala. The work
with the mental patients deepened his understanding of that power
of religious renewal and creativity which transcends and eludes
exhaustive rational analysis. This understanding greatly enhanced
his later work of interpretation in the fields of the Bible, the tradition
of the church, and the history of religions.

IN PARIS

About one year later Söderblom applied for the position of pastor to the Swedish legation in Paris, hoping that post would give him greater freedom and opportunity to establish his own household (he was married to Anna Forsell in the spring of 1894) and to pursue his studies at the Sorbonne. He received the appointment and served the Swedish congregation of Paris, as well as the Swedish sailors at Calais, from 1894 until 1901. In 1901 he completed his doctoral dissertation at the Sorbonne and was appointed soon thereafter (September 24, 1901) professor of "theological prenotions and encyclopedia" at the University of Uppsala.

The years as Swedish pastor in France were of great significance for Söderblom's life and thought. His biographer, Tor Andrae, was right in saying that the equipment of Söderblom's ecumenical mind was greatly enhanced by his ability to speak fluently the language of international discourse, and to gain an intimate knowledge of the culture of France and of Paris. During his years in Paris Söderblom was deeply impressed by Tolstoy's protest against war, and Tolstoy's novels and dramatic writings about the Gospels opened Söderblom's eyes to the revolutionary character of the teachings of Jesus. Out of this experience grew his book entitled *Jesus' Sermon on the Mount and Our Time* (1898), in which he challenged the prevailing ethos of the culture-Protestantism of his day. His treatment of current moral and social questions in the light of the eschatological figure of the Jesus of the Sermon on the Mount has a remarkable spiritual kinship to Albert Schweitzer's epoch-making work on *The Quest of the Historical Jesus,* published eight years later, in 1906.

In Paris and Calais Söderblom became involved in social work among the Swedish inhabitants of France. Especially in Paris the pastor was respected because he was actively promoting the social betterment of his people. He learned from this experience a lesson for the rest of his life: practical Christianity emphasizes faith active in love and good works; it is not interested in judging men by the standards of orthodoxy or pietism. A movement in Söderblom's career as theologian and churchman was initiated here which reached its climax at the Stockholm Conference on Life and Work in 1925, one of the predecessors of the present World Council of Churches and at many points closely related in spirit to the moral and social renewal of Roman Catholicism that was initiated at the Second Vatican Council in Rome. His attitude toward practical Christianity did not mean that right action is important and right belief irrelevant to the life of the church. He was very much concerned for the truth of the Christian faith. But he saw that the Christianity of his day was like a drowning man. His first Christian duty was to pull him out, and not to interrogate him about his views. It was Söderblom's radical response to crisis.

Despite the range of his interests and duties in the French capital, Söderblom kept in close touch with the theological climate of his native Sweden. The liberal theology of Ritschl was beginning to gain a foothold in the Swedish universities about the turn of the century and caused much alarm among theologians and pastors. Söderblom was convinced that if Swedish theology was to make a creative contribution to the theology of the twentieth century, it would have to face Ritschlian liberalism, to wrestle with the questions it raised, and to find its own creative answers. He therefore rose to the defense of Ritschlian theology and academic freedom when it was suggested by the court preacher of the king of Sweden that no students who were influenced by Ritschlianism should be permitted to pass examinations leading to an academic degree in theology. His defense of Ritschlianism and liberalism alienated many church people in Sweden and caused the young Söderblom to be largely isolated at the Swedish church in Paris. The wisdom of Söderblom's courageous stand was demonstrated by subsequent developments which made Ritschl's influence pervasive both in Europe and America. The theology of Karl Barth, for instance, cannot be adequately understood without reference to the Ritschlian School.

Meanwhile Söderblom continued to serve his congregation in Paris and to study at the Protestant divinity school of the Sorbonne. In 1899 he published a work on *The Fravashis,* or guardian angels of Mazdaism, in which he showed that these angels go back to an ancient, primitive belief in the power of the dead. By the end of the next year his doctoral dissertation on *The Future Life According to*

Mazdaism was ready. Both of these works were reviewed favorably by leading scholars, theologians, and historians of religion (e.g., the French Reformed theologian and philosopher of religion Auguste Sabatier, the French Roman Catholic orientalist and biblical critic Abbé Alfred Loisy, and the world-renowned authority in comparative religion, C. P. Tiele, professor at Leiden, Netherlands). Söderblom received his doctoral degree, and the quality of his work established his international reputation as an authority in the history of religions.

The years of study and experience at the Sorbonne in Paris strengthened Söderblom's ecumenical spirit and brought about a fresh appreciation of the liturgical tradition of the church. He was helped by the symbolism of the so-called Paris School under Auguste Sabatier to become more fully aware of the fact that human words and ideas cannot fully express the divine, and that therefore the artistic, liturgical, and doctrinal expressions of the faith of the church are symbolical in nature. As Jesus had shown, one of the best ways to talk about the realities of faith is to speak in parables. The life, power, and truth of God are universal, but this universality is hidden under the covering of historically and culturally conditioned symbolical expressions. Since the ancient creeds and traditions of the church are parabolic and symbolic in nature, just as our creeds and traditions today are at best of symbolic character, it is possible to value the ancient and in many ways obsolete confessions and liturgies of the church. Söderblom's inclination toward cherishing and preserving the historical tradition of the church was thus strengthened. It helped him to rediscover the evangelical as well as the catholic heritage of the Church of Sweden, which under his leadership became a bridge and meeting place between evangelical and Protestant churches on the one hand, and Anglo-Catholics as well as Greek Catholic churches on the other. He thus helped to pave the way to the eventual union of Orthodox and Protestants in the World Council of Churches.

AS PROFESSOR

In 1901 Söderblom was called to become professor of theology at the University of Uppsala. He accepted the call and tried to implement a program which called for more freedom and greater efforts to relate religious faith and scientific research constructively. His work as professor and scholar ushered in something like a new spirit in Swedish theology. At a time when Swedish theological education was dominated by German theological influence, he had the courage and vision to devote a whole year to the study of nineteenth-century Swedish theology and to the relationship between Protestantism and Roman Catholicism. Out of these reflections grew his book on *Religious Problems in Catholicism and Protestantism* (1910). Söderblom's broad ecumenical vision and his international reputation as scholar, historian of religions, and theologian enabled him, in cooperation with his younger colleague at the University of Uppsala, Einar Billing, to lay the foundations for the growth of an independent and internationally important Swedish school of theology. The historian of religions Tor Andrae and the theologian Gustaf Aulén both studied under Söderblom. Gustaf Aulén's great dogmatic work, *The Faith of the Christian Church*, has become a standard textbook of theology in Lutheran seminaries around the world. Andrae's contributions to the study of Islam have won international recognition. Known the world over is also the book *Agape and Eros* by Einar Billing's student Anders Nygren, the outstanding representative of Swedish Lundensian motif-research. Together with men like Gustaf Wingren, whose Luther studies and theological creativity have been internationally recognized, Aulén, Andrae, and Nygren have redeemed the promise of the pioneering thrust of the Söderblom-Billing theological constellation.

The lasting and most valuable contributions of Söderblom to the theological revival at Uppsala at the beginning of the twentieth century are chiefly three. First, the field of comparative religion and the history of religions has attained to a stronger position as a subject of study than in any other country and thus has made considerable contributions to the growth and style of Swedish theology. For example, the theologian Anders Nygren began as a lecturer under Eduard Lehmann, professor of comparative religion at the University of Lund, but not as a lecturer in theology. Likewise, the theologian Gustaf Aulén began as a lecturer under Nathan Söderblom, and also not as a lecturer in theology.

Second, both Söderblom and Billing had a great interest in seeking to establish the uniqueness of Christian revelation in the context of other religious and philosophical systems. Söderblom's important early essay on *The Nature of Revelation* (1903) pioneered the theme and partly also the method of this inquiry into what the distinctive character of Christianity consists of. Söderblom answered that the uniqueness of genuine Christianity is the historical and personal character of divine revelation, and with important variations this is the main theme of Swedish theology in the twentieth century.

Third, the legacy of Söderblom and Billing has stimulated a continuing interest in the study of Martin Luther. Söderblom himself was occupied with Luther studies almost without interruption, and references to Luther permeate many of his writings. In addition, he published two books on the life and thought of Luther, *Humor and Melancholy and Other Luther Studies* (1919) and *Martin Luther's Small Catechism* (2nd edition, 1929), in which he emphasized the uniqueness and universality of the religious genius of Martin Luther.

Besides his position of theological professor at the University of Uppsala, Söderblom was also pastor *(prebendekyrkoherde)* at *Trefaldighetskyrkan* (Trinity Church) of Uppsala. His preaching had a special appeal for the university community, and attendance at his services was extraordinarily large. At a time when there was a marked decline in church attendance in Sweden, this astonishing result was brought about to some degree by his captivating way of celebrating the liturgy, but also to a large degree by the power of his sermons, which aroused in his listeners the feeling that a renewal of the church was beginning to take place. In his view of the revelation of the living God through Scripture and tradition in the church, he was truly catholic in the original and profound sense of the term. He stressed the universality and continuity of the process of revelation in the church through saints and creative geniuses who manifest the power of the living God continuously at work in nature, history, and human personality. His feeling for oneness with the saints of the past was very vivid. At the anniversary of the death of Saint Eric it was his custom to go to Uppsala Cathedral and to pray at the tomb of the saint. He did the same on the anniversary days of the death of the Archbishop of the Swedish Reformation, Laurentius Petri, and other Christian and Lutheran saints.

While professor at Uppsala, Söderblom stimulated interest in closer ties with the Church of England. He pointed out that for a theologian there was something worth learning in the experience of the Church of England, and he picked up the suggestion made at the Lambeth Conferences of 1888 and 1897 that the Church of Sweden with its unbroken apostolic succession offered possibilities for closer cooperation. When, before the Lambeth Conference of 1908, inquiries were made with Archbishop Ekman of Sweden, Söderblom encouraged the commencement and continuation of negotiations between the two parties. He persuaded Ekman, who was minded to reject the British invitation, to send Bishop H.-W. Tottie to England as head of the delegation of the Church of Sweden. Tottie's mission resulted in continued study of the relationship between the Churches of Sweden and England. Thanks largely to the far-sighted and creative persistence of Söderblom's efforts at the conference table and through publications, the negotiations were successful. In 1922 intercommunion between the Church of England and the Church of Sweden was authorized by both sides.

A decisive event in the development of Söderblom's ecumenical vision was his presence, in 1911, at the World Student Christian Federation meeting in Constantinople. In his book *Three Holy Weeks* he recorded some of his thoughts about the union between the Orthodox East and the Protestant West which became a vivid experience for him during his stay in Constantinople. He especially rejoiced that at the meeting students of the Orthodox Church had been brought into the World Student Christian movement, thus giving it a more truly ecumenical character. The presence of Orthodox Christians also facilitated the cooperation with Anglicans of high-church sentiments.

DUAL PROFESSORSHIPS

In 1912 Söderblom was appointed professor at the University of Leipzig, Germany. From that time on, until the outbreak of World War I in 1914, he held two professorships, one at Leipzig and one at Uppsala. Two of the greatest scholars at Leipzig, the church historian Albert Hauck and the biblical scholar Rudolf Kittel, had recommended him because of his ability to bring out more clearly the uniqueness of Christianity through the study of the history of religions. He challenged the validity of Adolf von Harnack's authoritative view that the history of religions had nothing to do with theology and belonged therefore in the department of philosophy.

Söderblom's ability to integrate successfully the study of non-Christian religions into the discipline of theology was one of his great contributions. In his essay on *The Historian of Religions and the Church Theologian* he laid the theoretical foundation for a fruitful relationship between theology and the history of religions. He showed how the study of non-Christian religions in historical perspective helps to bring out more clearly what is genuinely Christian. The genius of Christianity is its historical character and emphasis, so that to the degree that we move away from the human person to a yearning for absorption into the abstract, metaphysical One, we move away from what is genuinely Christian. The center of Christianity is the living God revealing himself in and through historical events and human persons, and supremely in the life and vicarious suffering of Jesus Christ. In his essay on *Natural Religion and the History of Religions* he argued that from now on the history of religions must take the place which traditional theology had assigned to natural theology. All religion is historical and concrete; there is no empirically verifiable religion that could be called a universal, natural religion. The traditional notion of natural theology is an abstract and unscientific figment of the imagination which contradicts the historical character of all religion. Once the history of religions has replaced the imaginary natural religion, it will not only fill the vacuum left by the demise of the obsolete notion of natural religion, but will also enable Christianity to relate itself to the concrete and living historical religions of today in a way which the unrealistic notion of natural religion did not permit.

During his time at the University of Leipzig, Söderblom sought to make a creative contribution to the advancement of knowledge by breaking down the strict walls of separation between the various fields of academic inquiry. He was profoundly aware of the interrelatedness of all reality and thus also of all fields of knowledge. At the time, his efforts to further dialogue and the creation of inter- disciplinary fields of inquiry were met with little understanding. But today his appreciation of the relatedness of the various fields of study has been vindicated, and the emergence of such fields of study as biochemistry indicate the farsighted wisdom of Nathan Söderblom's interdisciplinary perspective. Also the trend to build theological schools and seminaries near great centers of learning rather than, as was formerly done, away from them in the isolation of a rural or small town setting, indicates that Söderblom's understanding of the need of each field of knowledge to learn from the others and to be in continual dialogue with them is being received more favorably.

While professor at Leipzig, Söderblom lived through a period of great creativity. He wrote his great book on *The Genesis of Belief in God,* which went through two editions in Germany. In this work he showed the continuity of the religion of the Old Testament with nonbiblical religions. At the same time he sought to specify what made the religion of the Jews different from, and unique among, the religions of the world. Finally, he stressed the awesome, unpredict- able, yet merciful power of the Lord of Israel, the God of Abraham, of Moses, and of the prophets.

During the Leipzig period also appeared Söderblom's remarkable essay on *General and Primitive Holiness* (1913), in which he deline- ated the essential and most basic element of all religion: holiness. It is noteworthy that he preceded by several years Rudolf Otto's world famous book on *The Idea of the Holy* (1917), which developed essentially the same discovery through the study of comparative re- ligion and the history of religions. This discovery was that the idea of the holy is more basic to religion than anything else, more basic even than the idea of God. That which distinguished Söderblom's essay on *Holiness* from Otto's *Idea of the Holy* was Söderblom's greater sensitivity to the genuinely religious in other religions and to the uniquely Christian in biblical religion. This deeper apprecia- tion of, and commitment to, the truly religious core of each of the various religions of the world helped Söderblom to avoid Otto's rationalistic and psychologizing interpretation of the holy, which tended to discredit Otto's discovery in the eyes of many theologians and made it actually impossible to incorporate the idea of holiness into the creative process of theological reconstruction in the twentieth century. In this and a number of other respects Söderblom's work with the concept of the holy was theologically superior to Otto's, but because of the predominance of German theology and because of the Swedish language barrier, the fuller development of Söderblom's concept of holiness did not receive the attention it deserved.

ARCHBISHOP

In 1914, shortly before the outbreak of World War I, Söderblom was elected Archbishop of Uppsala and thus Primate of the Church of Sweden. The choice came as a great surprise to him and to most Swedes, because among the three candidates for the office Söderblom was considered the third choice. But the seventeen years during which he occupied the highest spiritual office in Sweden were among the most active and exciting in the entire history of the Church of Sweden. For him the most important thing about the office of archbishop was not an abstract concept or a list of duties, but the power and dynamic action of the personality which filled the office, gave it life, and made it a living witness to the eternal voice of God in the contemporary world. Söderblom was a tireless worker who never spared himself when he was doing the Lord's work. It was for him better to work oneself to death than to rust to death. He was involved in hundreds of details almost at the same time, visiting churches, organizing conferences, and directing the international as well as the national affairs of the Church of Sweden. To well-meaning friends, who warned him that at the pace he was going he would kill himself, he replied that he would gladly sacrifice his life for the church and God's work. The Christian must be ready like a faithful soldier to fall in the line of duty.

Söderblom did everything in his power to renew the life of the Church of Sweden. Appeals to the nation were made by him in order to raise extra money so that many deserted village churches could be renovated and reopened. He tried to enrich the Swedish hymnal with hymns and spiritual folk songs from the evangelical revival in Sweden, because many of these songs were dear to the people.

They had devotional warmth and genuinely powerful piety and in Söderblom's view would have been most suited to bring the people back to church and make them feel at home in it. The hymns of the church are always in process, and he was convinced that new and popular hymns must constantly be added if the hymnal were to remain a vital force in Swedish church life. As a catholic churchman, the archbishop sought to enhance the worship of the church with the riches of ecclesiastical tradition and ancient Christian usages. The elaborate ritual, ecclesiastical pomp, and magnificent celebrations of worship which he revived were sometimes the object of criticism. But he reminded his critics of the rich and historical continuity of the Church of Sweden, which preserved the apostolic succession through the storms of the Reformation. The traditional forms of worship gave added dignity and a wider scope to the religious style of the church's contemporary life.

The first four years of Söderblom's career as archbishop were filled with the terror of the First World War. Although safe in neutral Sweden, he suffered greatly under the fact that the Body of Christ was being torn asunder and tormented by Christians whose eyes had been blinded by hatred, chauvinism, and self-righteous indignation. Already a few weeks after the outbreak of the war, he issued an appeal to the Christian leaders of Europe to unite in a common Christian appeal for peace. Then he worked to bring about a universal Christian conference uniting the Christian leaders of the warring nations in a common search for peace. But both times the religious leaders were either unwilling or unable to join in a common, united effort to bring peace to a war-torn world. With undaunted courage Söderblom continued his work for world peace both during and after the war. In recognition of his efforts to promote the noble cause of universal peace he was awarded the Nobel Peace Prize in 1930.

AS ECUMENICAL CATALYST

Closely related to Söderblom's work for universal world peace was his unfailing endeavor to bring together the many churches into one dynamic instrument of Christian world opinion and world action. The social and moral concerns of an international, ecumenical movement, which later grew to a climax in the Life and Work movement under the leadership of Söderblom, received a tremendous impetus through the war. He was interested in the Faith and Order movement which had grown out of the Edinburgh Conference of 1910 and was led by Bishop Brent of the Protestant Episcopal Church in the U.S. But his primary attention was devoted to the social and moral concerns of the ecumenical Life and Work movement.

The culmination of the pioneering ecumenical endeavors of the Life and Work movement was the Stockholm Conference of 1925, when Anglicans, Protestants, and Orthodox Christians met in one of the most impressive gatherings of the ecumenical movement in the twentieth century. The Orthodox Patriarch Photios of Alexandria was the most illustrative representative of the Eastern Orthodox churches, whereas the strongest Protestant delegation was sent by German Lutheranism. Anglicanism was represented by high as well as by low church men.

The central factor and uniting element at the ecumenical Stockholm Conference was Jesus Christ. The foundation was thus laid for the future ecumenical creed of the World Council of Churches, which in 1961, at New Delhi, defined itself as "a fellowship of churches which confess the Lord Jesus Christ as God and Saviour according to the Scriptures and therefore seek to fulfill together their common calling to the glory of the one God, Father, Son, and Holy Spirit." The unifying force of Christianity was thus seen to be Jesus Christ, the central mystery of the faith. Christian unity, as Söderblom had insisted, must begin at the center of the faith of the Christian church. The farther the movement of ecumenism progresses, the more clearly the wisdom and insight of his ecumenical vision stands out.

A second important emphasis of the ecumenical Stockholm Conference was the responsibility of the Christian community for the welfare of the neighbor, the nation, and the world. Andrae rightly says in his Söderblom biography that for the archbishop the central question was that of the nature of the kingdom of God and the rule of God in today's world. Even though this question did not appear in print as a discussion topic, in much of the discussion at Stockholm

Statue of Söderblom near Eisenach, Germany.

Nathan Söderblom's father, Pastor Jonas Söderblom, and mother, Sofia.

The room in the Tröno, Sweden, parsonage where tradition says Nathan Söderblom was born January 15, 1866.

Exterior of the Tröno parsonage now preserved as a museum.

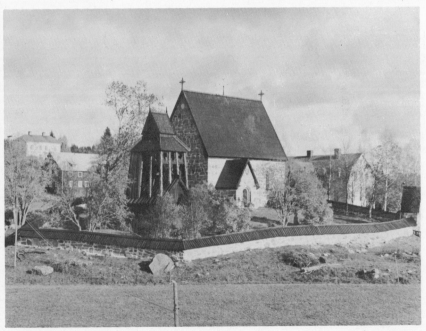

Church in Tröno, Sweden, where Söderblom's father was pastor at the time Nathan was born.

Pastor and Mrs. Jonas Söderblom with one-year-old Nathan.

Nathan Söderblom, seated right, as a confirmand in 1881 with his brother Svante.

Söderblom as a 17-year-old student.

Söderblom in 1893, a student at the University of Uppsala.

Right: Three University of Uppsala comrades—Nathan Söderblom, Herman Palmgren, and Anshelm Berglöf.

Below: Group photo taken at the 1890 World Student Missionary Conference at the home of Dwight L. Moody in Northfield, Mass. Söderblom, a University of Uppsala delegate, is seated in the foreground, lower left.

The newly-married Nathan and Anna Söderblom.

The young Professor Söderblom speaking at a spring festival at Uppsala University.

The Söderblom family in 1905 when he was a professor at Uppsala University.

A Christmas portrait of the Söderbloms in the Archbishop's palace in Uppsala.

Archbishop Söderblom's study in the episcopal palace.

Archbishop Nathan Söderblom, primate of the Lutheran Church of Sweden, in episcopal vestments.

Above: Söderblom, author of more than 700 books and articles, at his desk in 1924.

Right: The two recipients, Söderblom and Kellogg, await the presentation of the 1930 Nobel Peace Prize.

Right: Söderblom at helm of motor boat on trip across Gulf of Finland in 1922.

Above: Söderblom at Augustana Theological Seminary, Rock Island, Ill., in 1923.

Right: Söderblom visiting the famous Swedish author, Selma Lagerlöf, at Mårbacka.

Patriarch Photios and Söderblom at the Stockholm Ecumenical Conference in 1925.

Söderblom at the Gustavus-Adolphus festival in Stralsund, Germany.

One of Söderblom's concerns was for better understanding among world religions. Here he is shown with Indian Mystic Sundar Singh.

Söderblom, left, with the Lord Bishop of London at the Stockholm Conference of 1925.

Söderblom holding his grandchild, a picture taken five days before his death on July 12, 1931.

The two first citizens of Sweden, Archbishop Söderblom and King Gustav, at the dedication of St. Ansgar's Chapel in 1930.

Above: The archbishop's funeral procession moves from the episcopal palace to Uppsala Cathedral across the street, July 18, 1931.

The Söderblom funeral service inside the cathedral.

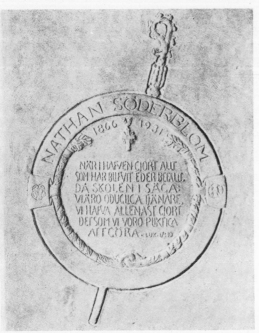

Left: The emblem on the Söderblom tomb in Uppsala Cathedr
inscribed with a favorite verse
"When you have done all that
commanded you, say, 'We are un
worthy servants; we have only don
what was our duty.'" Luke 17:1

Below: The ancient Lutheran (
thedral of Uppsala, seat of Swed
archbishops for centuries.

the center of attention focused on it. Two tendencies emerged in the course of the conference. On the one hand was the Lutheran point of view, dominated by the strong German delegation. It expressed the conviction that the kingdom will never be realized in this world. All attempts to establish the rule of God on earth are in the final analysis illusory. There is no shortcut around individual personal commitment to Christ and his church on the part of every man. A program of building the kingdom can only too easily degenerate into mere activism and superficial socializing without any real connection to the essential faith of the church and to the belief in divine guidance in the contemporary world.

On the other hand the representatives of Anglo-Saxon Christianity of the Reformed tradition sponsored the view that the kingdom of God is essentially a program for Christian social action. The creation of interdenominational committees and practical cooperation between Christians can bring about a renewal of the world in accordance with the will of God. The task is immense, but faith can move mountains. Christ is with us and he can give his servants the strength to accomplish the seemingly impossible.

Söderblom understood that the conflict of these two views of the kingdom of God was between two tendencies which needed each other. The ecumenical movement was for him the process in which Lutheran and Anglo-Saxon Reformed Protestants mutually enriched and enhanced one another. By coming together as two trends in one dynamic movement of ecumenism, each could serve as the corrective of the other. The archbishop combined both in himself, the inner-directedness of the one, and the active Christian love and outreach of the other. He was a firm and committed Lutheran ecumenist who had learned much of the practical inclination of Anglo-Saxon Christianity.

The two strands of inner-directed and outer-directed Christian love in the ecumenical context have continued to stand in creative and fruitful tension in the Life and Work movement and now in the World Council of Churches. Söderblom's vision of the necessity of a new ecumenical creed of the churches, in which the two strands of Christian concern would be freely and creatively united, remains to this day a real challenge and significant guideline for the future development and process of Christian unity.

A third point of major significance which occupied the ecumenical gathering at Stockholm was the issue of world peace. The threat of another and even more devastating world war hung over the 1925 conference at Stockholm as it hangs over us today. The concern of many ecumenical churchmen and theologians at Stockholm was awakened by the awareness that the churches were partly responsible for the wars of the past as well as for the threat of the next war. The churches had in the past failed, with few exceptions, to take a united and uncompromising stand for peace and against war. Söderblom and his fellow ecumenists in the Life and Work movement were spurred on by their Christian consciences to stress the role of the churches as champions of peace whose effective witness depends in large measure on their unity. Under his influence the cause of world peace and the cause of Christian unity through ecumenism became welded together into a new dynamic unity. The vitality of the Söderblomian vision of ecumenism and peace has today spread to all the churches that are involved in the movement of ecumenism. The present world situation will make this vision most relevant both in the immediate and in the more distant future as the ecumenical spirit progressively inspires the churches more and more to unite in a common willingness to assume together, and as one ecumenical church, the responsibility of Christian faith and love for the care of the earth.

Despite his arduous tasks as archbishop, Söderblom found time to continue to write in theology, church history, and the history of religions. His prominent role in the spiritual and intellectual life of Sweden and the world was given recognition by his election to the Swedish Academy of Sciences in 1921, and by the invitation to give the famous Gifford Lectures at Edinburgh in 1931. These lectures were published posthumously under the title *The Living God*, and constitute the last great work of Söderblom, a work which has ever since been of considerable interest to historians of religion as well as theologians.

A few weeks following his lectures, on July 12, 1931, Söderblom died after a short illness. He was buried next to Archbishop Lars in the Cathedral of Uppsala in special recognition of his outstanding service to the Church of Sweden and to the ecumenical church of the future. Not for about one hundred years had a Swede received similar honor. Yet even in death the archbishop remained the humble servant of Christ and of the church catholic. According to his instructions the following words from Luke 17:10 were read at the grave and are now inscribed on Söderblom's tombstone: "So you also, when you have done all that is commanded you, say, 'We are unworthy servants; we have only done what was our duty.'"

CHAPTER IV

SÖDERBLOM AND LUTHER

In the preceding biographical survey of Söderblom's life and work, reference was made to his continued, life-long study of Luther's writings. The archbishop had inherited this interest from his father, and it had been broadened through his study of Albrecht Ritschl's (at that time novel and forbidden) approach to Luther studies. Söderblom, and many other brilliant students at the University of Uppsala, had discovered in Luther the liberating air of authentic reformatory passion. Disgusted by the stuffy, dead orthodoxy of Swedish Lutheranism in the 1880's and 1890's, and fired by the evangelical spirit of Luther, they began to criticize the established orthodoxy of Uppsala Lutheranism in the name of the original ideas and ideals of Luther's Reformation. The evangelical and catholic vision of Martin Luther became for Söderblom the unfathomable object of ceaseless fascination.

It is no exaggeration to say that among all the figures in the history of Christian thought no one had greater significance for the life and thought of Söderblom than Luther. Throughout his entire lifetime Archbishop Söderblom continued to study the works of Luther with ever fresh enthusiasm. He drew, from these almost inexhaustible writings, an evangelical profundity and a catholic universality without which, we may safely assume, he would not have become one of the great ecumenical leaders of the twentieth century. His love and respect for Luther was greater than that for any other man, and since faithful and genuine love is the indispensable condition for true understanding, there was no one whom he understood more truly than Martin Luther. And no one in the history of the Christian church exerted a more profound and decisive influence on Söderblom than the evangelical reformer.

In his essay entitled *Why I Am a Lutheran,* Söderblom hails Luther as the greatest religious genius since Paul. He characterizes him as a man consumed by an ultimate passion for inner peace with God and saving, divine truth. Certainly Luther looms before him as the guardian angel of evangelical faith. But it is this very admiration for Martin Luther that makes him hesitant to call himself a Lutheran. One of the reasons for his hesitation is his recognition of the wisdom of Luther's own warning to his friends and followers not to call themselves after him whose mortal body would soon be a bag of worms. If they wanted to be one with him in spirit and in truth they should be happy and content to call themselves simply Christians.

The other reason is his self-awareness as an evangelical catholic. His ecumenical self-consciousness rebels against the sectarian connotation of the designation "Lutheran." In the opening lines of his *Why I Am a Lutheran* (the publisher of the volume in which his essay appeared had insisted that he write it with this title) he raises the question, "Am I a Lutheran?" Söderblom's answer is typical of his ecumenical and evangelical sensibilities. He replies by stressing what to him is of first importance: his being a member of the *una sancta catholica et apostolica ecclesia,* the One Holy Catholic and Apostolic Church. Then he points out that he, and the other people called "the Lutherans," are quite self-consciously heirs of the spiritual and ecumenical faith of the apostle Paul, but do not for this reason call themselves Paulists or Paulinians.

The same is true of the Nicene Creed and its great champion St. Athanasius. "The Lutherans" firmly adhere to this catholic statement of the faith of the church, yet do not call themselves Athanasians. Likewise they find in Saint Augustine's existential statement of the sovereignty of divine love and the impotence of human sin the most relevant expression of the Gospel of grace between the apostle Paul and the Reformation in the sixteenth century. Yet they do not therefore call themselves Augustinians. They rejoice in the blessed light of divine love that radiated from the humble life and work of St. Francis of Assisi and that made him the greatest Christian of the Middle Ages. Nevertheless, they would not think of calling themselves Franciscans. They wholeheartedly accept the priceless message of evangelical confidence and liberty which God proclaimed through his chosen prophet Martin Luther, whose spiritual stature and religious genius have not been equalled since New Testament times. But unfortunately, through custom and historical necessity they first were called, and now proudly call themselves, "Lutherans."

The name "Lutheran" is unfortunate not only because it contradicts directly and openly the express teaching of Luther himself and debases the Reformation to the level of a sectarian party label, but also because it knowingly defies the explicit injunction of the apostle Paul, who in the third chapter of First Corinthians openly criticized the Corinthian custom of naming Christian groups after Paul or Cephas or Apollos. But if it is necessary to use what Söderblom calls "a special sect-name," then there is some merit in making the name of one of the great servants of the living God and his Christ into the proper name of a sect, because the ineffable, luminous quality of the religious mystery is more easily understood when incarnate in a human form than if it is enshrined in a sacred formula. After all, he says, there are Christian groupings which call themselves after a place or a country as do the Greeks and Romans and the Anglicans. Then there are others who derive their names from special forms and expressions of religious piety, such as Methodists and Baptists. Finally, there are some who name themselves after their form of organization, e.g., Episcopalians or Presbyterians. Why not then use the name of one of God's great servants, which is so very expressive of the mystery of the Gospel, especially if this name belongs to the mightiest genius of religion since Paul? There are Wesleyans, Calvinists, Franciscans, and Benedictines—why not permit some such "sect-name" as "Lutheran"?

In his conclusion of *Why I Am a Lutheran* Söderblom proposes that the apparent necessity of custom which foists the name of the hero and genius of the Reformation, Martin Luther, on one of the subdivisions of Christianity can result in some unexpected good: the recovery of some essential aspects of the genuine, evangelical and catholic essence of Christianity. In the case of Lutherans it may bring about the restoration of a more truly evangelical and catholic conception of perfection, holiness, and sainthood. In contemporary Lutheranism there is a pervasive tendency to regard holiness and perfection in the sense of the absence of sins and faults, instead of a positive sense of great divine endowments and outstanding service in the church catholic. The Roman Catholic notion of sainthood, which is tied to the occurrence of supernatural miracles performed by the person who is to be canonized a saint, is quite primitive in its conception of religion and perhaps even incompatible with true Christianity. But this idea is still superior to the prevailing Protestant concept of a saint, because for Rome saintly perfection is the witness to, and result of, the power of divine grace, whereas the current Protestant idea of a saint rests on the absence of more or less obvious human imperfections, and thus on a predominantly negative understanding of holiness.

Is there a danger in Lutheranism that the cult of the personality of Luther becomes a substitute for the worship of Christ? Söderblom replies negatively to this question. He knows from his own experience that the more a man seriously immerses himself in the works of Luther, the more clearly the voice of the reformer directs him to Christ as his only Lord and Savior. The cross of Christ, the supreme symbol of human faithfulness and God's grace, stands out most clearly against the horizon of Luther's life and work, and the reformer himself obliges us to transcend all narrow and sectarian sympathies and to unite around the ecumenical center of Christianity, the holy cross.

The person of Martin Luther has, however, also a positive significance for contemporary Protestantism. In his remarkable book on the humor and melancholy of Luther *(Humor och melancholi och andra Lutherstudier)*, Söderblom advances the thesis that, apart from the inseparable relationship between Christianity and the person of Jesus of Nazareth, there is no achievement of world historical significance which is more intimately related to a leading personality than the Reformation is connected with the person, the life, and the work of Martin Luther. It is therefore not surprising, he remarks at the end of his book of Luther studies, that until this day there has been in every new century a more profound and adequate grasp of the significance of the Reformation for the religious and cultural history of the West, and for the entire world, and that this deepening of the understanding of the Reformation period has been accompanied by an increasingly high estimate of Martin Luther. Söderblom underscores the evolution of what he believes to be a revolution in the Roman Catholic interpretation of Luther as a definite indication that this process will gather new momentum in the twentieth century.

Further, the ecumenical movement will bring with it an increased interest in Luther's works. Söderblom stresses the ecumenical significance of Luther and the essentially catholic, that is ecumenical and anti-sectarian, message of the Reformation. In his 1917 *Greeting to the American Lutheran Church in View of the 400th Anniversary of the Reformation,* he points out that through Martin Luther's work "we see the blessings of the Reformation for the true consolation of poor human souls; for the purity, strength and richness of faith; for the sanctity of duty; for the glory of faithfulness in human relations and in the fulfilment of different human vocations; for the individual, for the commonwealth, for civilization, for humanity." The awareness of the immensity of the grace of God in Christ and the consciousness of the blessing of justification by grace through faith are the heritage of God's prophet and evangelist Martin Luther, which is meant to be a blessing to all of Christendom and not just for those who call themselves Lutherans. The three great *solas* of the Reformation, *sola gratia, sola per fidem, sola propter Christum,* by grace alone, through faith alone, only because of Christ, are Luther's last will and testament for all Christians, and if those who are called Lutherans feel themselves to stand in a special relationship to these great touchstones of evangelical catholicity, it must be in the form of a heightened sense of their special calling within the whole of Christendom.

It would be a disastrous mistake, Söderblom warned, to understand the three *solas* as infallible dogmas or timeless truths. In his book on Martin Luther's *Small Catechism (Martin Luthers lilla katekes)* Söderblom emphasizes that the recovery of the real essence of Christianity which took place through Luther and the Reformation would be robbed of its power and relevance if the saving truth of Christian faith were to be abstracted from history and transformed into a universal, timeless truth. Christian revelation is always bound up with the process of life, with personal and world history.

Salvation by grace through faith is meaningless as a timeless, universal truth, and meaningful only as it becomes real in existential concrescence. God redeems man not from history but in history, not from involvement in inter-human responsibilities but for greater love and freedom and faithfulness in his religious and secular duties before God and fellow men. God's love and mercy because of Christ and for Christ's sake is not love in general, but love in concrete, individual instances at a particular time and a particular place in the personal life of the individual and in the history of the nation and the world. And the response of the Christian to the love of God through a life of loyal service and humble obedience to God is not the response of service and obedience in general, but in particular, concrete decisions which are ever new and thus continually challenge our creativity and devotion. Luther's Christianity is not a set of universal, timeless truths ready at hand for our use like a bottle of pills for every illness, so that we need only to take it from the shelf and apply it as a universal remedy. It is rather a process of growth in which successive phases evolve in the concreteness of personal and historical existence. Every person and every generation in history must struggle anew to recover the evangelical and catholic vision of Luther, in whom the lines traversed by the evolution of revelation converge to form a focus of rare power and kerygmatic insight. His epoch-making discovery of the evangelical freedom of the Christian man as a member of Christ's one holy catholic flock on earth is a concrete, personal experience transferable only through the *via fidei* of personal mysticism (*personlighetsmystik*).

In his essay on *Luther in the Light of Ecumenicity (Luther im Lichte der Ökumenizität)* Söderblom takes issue with three common misunderstandings of Luther. The first is that Luther was the man who used the most violent language against the Pope and the Roman See. This popular point of criticism is justified. Even Luther's wife, Katherine von Bora, sometimes objected to his coarse cursing. He knew it himself but said that the heavy armor he used would cause less suffering and pain than the constant needling of others. But if we read the literature of the first half of the sixteenth century, it is surprising that in all of Luther's writings there is none of that frivolity which is not uncommon in the works of his contemporaries, including the great Erasmus.

A second popular misapprehension is that Luther exalted faith at the expense of good works. This is not true. Luther denounced the work-righteousness of special exercises of piety, but he emphasized the necessary ethical exercise of love and justice in human relations. The real demands of faith were vastly increased, rather than decreased, by Luther, because faith is no real faith if it does not involve the total, faithful self-surrender in the service of the neighbor. No religious or ascetic exercises can free us from the inescapable divine command to love our neighbor.

A third misunderstanding of the work of Martin Luther is the idea that with the reformer originated the rebellion of human reason and human will against the authority of God and of the church. Söderblom notes with satisfaction that twentieth-century Roman Catholic Luther scholars have resolutely rejected this idea as patently false. Quite the opposite is true. In Luther's vision of Christianity, human reason and human will have lost all of their claims to power in a way that offers a radical criticism of natural theology as well as of the prudently balanced mixture of reason and revelation, of grace and human merit, which dominated the medieval Roman moral and doctrinal theology. Today there is a general opinion among free-thinkers, as well as some Roman Catholics and Protestants, that Luther was a great fighter for human freedom who liberated the human spirit and reason from the oppressive authoritarianism of the Roman Church. In a 1921 speech, titled *The Four Hundredth Anniversary of Luther in Worms*, Söderblom repudiates this notion as completely false, as well as the related idea that Luther established a kind of rational middle way between the two extremes of freethinking and a tyrannical and corrupt church. The fact is that Luther belongs in the great succession of personality mystics which began with Paul and St. Augustine, whose characteristic trait was that they spoke freely and directly with God in their souls. We have only to read the Epistles of Paul, or the *Confessions* of St. Augustine or the *Theologia Germanica* edited by Luther, to realize that the Scriptures, St. Augustine, and the reformer are filled with the ardor of genuine personality mysticism. Here God is everything, man is nothing; here man is totally dependent upon the grace of God alone. And yet it is not a disintegrating, capricious subjectivism which is at work in Luther, but due to his total dependence on God the salvation of man is radically independent of human subjectivism, as objective and as firmly established as possible.

A number of pervasive themes run through all of Söderblom's studies of Luther. These motifs also recur in his other theological and devotional writings and are a testimony of how for Söderblom all these different strands of his thought converge in Martin Luther.

MYSTICISM

In his important and original essay on *The Religion of Revelation (Uppenbarelsereligion)* Söderblom works out his distinction between two basic types of mysticism, infinity mysticism and personality mysticism. Martin Luther is one of the primary examples for the latter type. His preoccupation with faith and confidence is an indication of the personal character of his mystical communion with God. Certainty of salvation rested for him on faith in Christ, and not on a fulfillment of the law or certain mystical experiences. Faith and confidence are personal dimensions, and these characterize the new life of the sinner in Christ.

In Luther's religion the identifying marks of the mysticism of personality are the terrors of conscience. These *terrores conscientiae* are the psychological manifestations of the radically ethical and personal nature of Luther's communion with God. They correspond, *mutatis mutandis,* to the *Frygt og Bæven,* the fear and trembling of the famous father of modern existentialism, Søren Kierkegaard. In his letter of January 13, 1522, Luther urged his right-hand man, Philip Melanchthon, to test all those prophets and *Schwärmer* of the Reformation period and determine *num experti sint spirituales illas angustias et nativitates divinas, mortes, infernosque,* if they have experienced spiritual tribulations and the divine birth pangs, death and hell. Experiences like these are the touchstone of genuine personality mysticism. But, said Luther to Melanchthon, *si audieris blanda, tranquilla, devota (ut vocant) et religiosa, etiamsi in tertium coelum sese raptos dicant, non approbabis,* that is, if you hear of pleasant delights, tranquillity, devotion (as they call it), and piety, you must reject them, even if they claim to have been exalted to the third heaven. Why? Because, according to Söderblom, these are the unmistakable symptoms of the mysticism of infinity, and thus alien to the real kerygma of the church, and the biblical mysticism of personality.

As we study the giants of personality mysticism, men like the prophet Jeremiah, the Apostle Paul, St. Augustine, Luther, Pascal, and Kierkegaard, we see men tremble under the mighty hand of God's grace, rather than the longing, dreaming gaze of the infinity mystic as he stretches out his hands toward that inexpressible holiness which is without name and form and lies beyond good and evil and on the other side of being and nonbeing. While the infinity mystic ascends to liberty in the ineffable spaces of infinity, the personality mystic wrestles with his God on the brink of the abyss of death. He trembles and bleeds as a burning sense of personal guilt before God consumes his soul. Only as he knows himself in the mighty hand of God can he defy sin, death, and the devil. Luther's *terrores* and *angustiae*, his terrors and fears, are characteristic marks of his personal communion with God, and cannot be dismissed, as Ritschl and Harnack tried to do, as peculiar to Luther's special situation and the ignorance of salvation by grace through faith in which he had been held by the medieval penitential system.

RELIGIOUS GENIUS

In his book on *Christian Fellowship* Söderblom describes Luther as a religious genius and evangelical mystic, in contrast to contemporaries such as Erasmus, who favored reform of the church's life and doctrine instead of an instructed and enlightened Christianity, and Ignatius Loyola with his mystical methods of training and his effective mobilization of Counter-Reformation forces in favor of the papal hierarchy. Loyola tended to stress methodical self-training, leading to mystical visions and ecstasies, whereas Luther's evangelical emphasis is dominated by the dialectic of man's sin and God's grace. The daily calling of the Christian in the world is true worship of God. The gracious activity of God creates in man heartfelt trust and confidence like that of a child. The ultimate confidence of Luther is grounded in the certainty of the grace of God and of the lordship of Jesus over his life. The salvation and peace which Luther desires above everything else cannot be attained by an effort of human reason or will, but are entirely the free gift of God. In the dialectic of sin and grace, guilt and forgiveness, monastic asceticism was of no help to Luther. Only the forgiving love of God could still the storms of fear that troubled his guilt-ridden soul; religious virtuosity and trained piety, such as championed by Loyola, could not help Luther.

Luther is the religious hero par excellence. The drama of the inner life of his soul becomes the arena in which the battle for the real essence of Christianity is fought out. Just as deeply rooted in medieval mysticism as Paul was rooted in Pharisaic religion, Luther consummates the evangelical vision of Paul and Augustine. Like Augustine he still operates against the mystical and Platonic dualism of soul and body, according to which the soul is free and happy in the spiritual realm, but the body forces the soul to get involved in the life of mankind and the world, in which it must be the servant of all in charity. This Augustinian antithesis forms the background of Luther's famous treatise *On Christian Liberty*. However, against this background he develops the dominant evangelical themes of trust in God, forgiveness of sins, and faithfulness in one's earthly calling. With him everything is spontaneous and direct, he has no patience with calculation and methodical training.

The effects of the work of the religious genius of Luther were not limited to the sixteenth century. Söderblom, in his book on *Christian Fellowship*, defends the thesis that in the life and work of John Wesley, the founder of Methodism, we find the Anglo-Saxon echo of Luther's Reformation doctrine of salvation by grace through faith. Luke Luther, Wesley had been nourished by the medieval mystical writings, especially those of Francis de Sales and the *Imitatio Christi* of Thomas à Kempis. Then the Moravian Brethren related to him Luther's religious discovery of evangelical trust and faith. The excesses of Moravianism alienated Wesley, and it was not until he heard Luther's own words that he experienced the decisive turning point in his life. When Wesley heard Luther's preface to the *Epistle to the Romans* read, his soul was captured by the liberating religious insight of the reformer, and the evangelical renewal swept England under the banner of Wesleyan Methodism.

To the question whether Methodism is basically Anglican, Reformed, or Lutheran, Söderblom replies that all three were welded by Wesley into one dynamic evangelical unity. With Luther's evangelical religious genius as a catalyst, Wesley's soul was moved by the Gospel to infuse new life into the lethargic Anglican church of his time, which had almost forgotten the Reformation spirit of genuine Christianity. Methodism is thus the genuine continuation of the Lutheran Reformation in the Anglo-Saxon world. It marks the creative impact of Luther's religious genius on an essentially Erasmian establishment.

SAINTS

In his lecture on the evangelical concept of a saint *(Der evangelische Begriff eines Heiligen)* Söderblom defines a saint as one who by his being and life shows that there is a living God whose power is manifest in human life. There are few great figures in the history of the church who are more worthy of the Söderblomian image of sainthood than Martin Luther, even though Luther himself protested against all attempts to make him a saint. In the last chapter of his book on *The Living God,* Söderblom demonstrates how Luther exhibits to an unsurpassed degree a characteristic common to many of the truly great saints of the church. This characteristic is that they reveal something of the nature of God himself through the grace and power with which their spirits are endowed. They demonstrate to their fellow men that the God and Father of our Lord Jesus Christ is ever-living and active in history and human personality. The originality and prophetic significance of Luther's creative insights are a dynamic testimony to the action of God in history at that particular time. The richness, power, and novel freshness of Luther's personality are a further witness to the continued revelation of the living God.

Söderblom notes that one of the marks of the greatest men who ever lived is their personal awareness of their own importance. Luther has this consciousness, in common with Socrates, Jesus, and

Paul. Already in a letter of January 25, 1521, addressed to the Elector of Saxony, Frederick the Wise, he draws attention to the fact that his work had promoted the blessedness and salvation of the whole of Christendom. A dozen years later Luther writes (in his preface to the defense against the charge of Duke George that he had engaged in treacherous agitation) that since biblical times no doctor of the church has instructed the laity so well and faithfully in the true religion of Christianity as he, Martin Luther. By the special grace of God he is even superior to St. Ambrose and St. Augustine, the time-honored experts of the enlightenment of the Christian conscience. Luther boasts of this in order to praise God's special providence and in order to defy and hurt the devil and all his tyrants and enemies. The insight of being specially favored by an extraordinary divine call does not make Luther arrogant and vain. His natural humility and his terrible struggles in the torments of the hell of despair and anguish, as well as his exultation and rejoicing in the mercy and forgiveness of God, his loving heavenly Father, bear witness to the fact that Luther was boasting of the gracious gifts which God had so lavishly bestowed upon him despite his unworthiness, and not of his own personal achievements. In this respect he follows the great procession of the saints of the church universal.

CONTINUED REVELATION

Söderblom is firmly convinced that revelation must be understood as ongoing process rather than something that happened only in the past and ended with the Bible. Christian faith is based on revelation, and its God is the living God who has never ceased to reveal himself. In his important essay on the interpretation of Christian faith and revelation (*Ett bidrag till den kristna uppenbarelsetrons tolkning*), Söderblom points out that at the time of the Reformation there existed a vivid consciousness that God in Luther revealed his saving truth and prophetic message. In a letter of 1537, Luther is hailed by Melanchthon as a prophet sent from God. In his lectures he contends that the doctrine of faith and forgiveness as proposed by Luther is a revelation of God through Luther, and not something speculative developed by the cleverness of the human mind. God, and not Luther himself, raised up the reformer as a prophetic voice of God's revelation.

The occasion of Luther's death at his native Eisleben, in 1546, gave opportunity to several outstanding leaders of the Reformation to give testimony of Luther's status as an outstanding agent in God's continued revelation. Dr. Jonas, for instance, observed that the death of God's great servants and prophets was often followed by great calamities and terrible divine judgments, because of the hardness of heart which rejects the prophetic message and often kills the prophets. The humanistic co-reformer, Melanchthon, declared that God's chosen servants, among whom Martin Luther stood out as one of the choicest flowers of true humanity, bear witness to the continued presence of God in his holy church. Bugenhagen, himself also a leading reformer, extolled Luther's high office as prophet and apostle of genuine Christianity, and saw in him the fulfillment of John Huss, the noble martyr of the Reformation. John Klajus of Herzberg contended that God, who spoke in Hebrew through Moses and the prophets, and in Greek through the apostles, chose Martin Luther and spoke in German through him. The contemporary artist Albrecht Dürer saw in Luther the fulfillment of biblical and medieval prophecies which pointed to the coming of a man of God upon whom the Spirit of God would rest in an extraordinary way, so that he would be a divinely inspired (gottgeistig) man.

The Formula of Concord, the last of the confessional and symbolical books of the Book of Concord, which forms the doctrinal foundation of the Lutheran Church, speaks of Luther as a man endowed by the Holy Spirit with gifts unique and most high, a man who foresaw in the Spirit things that were to come after his death. There was no doubt in the minds of the framers of the Formula that in Luther God had spoken again in their time as he spoke to his prophets and apostles from of old.

In an attempt to prove the continuance of divine revelation in the work of Luther, the orthodox scholastics of Lutheranism devoted a special locus in their dogmatics to the revelation of God through the life and work of Martin Luther. For example, the great doctor of Lutheran scholasticism, Johann Gerhard, made repeated reference to the special and divine call of Luther. In his great dogmatic work, the *Catholic Confession,* Gerhard refuted the papal idea that the Roman Church was the only true catholic church by showing how God's raising up of his servant Martin Luther constituted the foundation of the catholicity of the Reformation. At the centennial of the Reformation, in 1617, Gerhard wrote a special disputation on the divine call of Luther as reformer of the church catholic.

In his great systematic theology, the *Loci Theologici,* Gerhard returns frequently to the extraordinary call of Luther as the evangelical restorer and renovator of the church catholic. In Paragraph 84 of Chapter XXXI he refutes the papal allegation that Luther proclaimed an early judgment of the church and the world and therefore was a false prophet. In Paragraph 200 of Chapter XXV, which deals with the doctrine of the church, Gerhard defended against the Roman Cardinal Bellarmine the call of Luther as being both ordinary and extraordinary. Luther's call was regular, because he was regularly called and duly ordained to the priesthood in 1507, even though the ordaining bishop was irregular, and because he took the regular oath of a theological doctor of the church. Finally, Luther was regularly called to the University of Wittenberg, where he assumed the chair of theology in 1507. Cardinal Bellarmine argued that Luther's special and extraordinary call had to be proved by special miracles which he had performed. Gerhard rejoined that the way in which the reformer, without external force of arms, burst asunder the chains of the greatest power on earth, simply by the power of the Word of God and the weapons of the spirit and truth, was one of the greatest miracles of all time.

Gerhard proposed that Luther's reform of the church and his unmasking of the Antichrist went far beyond the ordinary call to the priesthood. There was a strong element of the extraordinary and unique in this work of Luther, which, together with biblical prophecies and the successful triumph of Luther's power and spirit-filled soul over the devil and his allies, made the reformer one of the foremost revealers and servants of God in the church, even though he did not have the same immediacy of divine calling which distinguished the prophets and apostles from all other men, and did not converse with the Holy Spirit as directly and powerfully as the prophets and apostles of biblical standing.

Gerhard advanced six proofs of the extraordinary call of Luther, which, though less extraordinary than that of the prophets and apostles, was far beyond that of the ordinary ordained servants of the church. The first proof consisted of biblical prophecies, such as Jer. 51:48; Dan. 11:44; Mal. 4:5; 2 Thess. 2:9; and Rev. 14:6, and of the Hussite prophecy of the coming reformer. Second were the extraordinary gifts of Luther, his unique spiritual insights into the simple essentials of Christian faith, the spiritual power of his writings, the miraculous ability to translate the Holy Scriptures, and his divine eloquence and great learning. A third proof was Luther's astonishing courage in the face of many and great dangers, a courage which was without doubt a special gift of God. Fourth was the reformer's miraculous escape from the treacherous violence of his enemies. Similar wonderful escapes by the grace and providence of God could be demonstrated in the lives of the prophets and apostles. A fifth proof of the special divine call of Luther to reform the church was the predictions of coming events which Luther made. Gerhard devoted a special essay to this topic and also made reference to them in Section 290 of the locus on the church in his *loci*. Sixth, and finally, there was the fact of the amazing progress and spread of the evangelical Reformation which, aided by the Word of God alone, successfully defied the papal and imperial powers of the world. "That Word above all earthly powers, no thanks to them, abideth," Luther wrote in the battle hymn of the Reformation, "A mighty fortress is our God."

Söderblom takes great pains to stress that Johann Gerhard was by no means the only Lutheran theologian of high standing who displayed a great deal of concern for, and appreciation of, the continuance of divine revelation through the life and work of Martin Luther. The outstanding Lutheran theologian Aegidius Hunnius called Luther's special place in the history of God's continued activity of revelation *heroica*, "heroic." *Heroica* had been used even before Hunnius' nomenclature as an attribute of the reformer's life and work. But now the word *heroica* received a special meaning in

Lutheran theological discourse and was reserved to designate an extraordinary position halfway between the apostles and other servants of the church universal. The *heroica* call made Luther's place in the continued revelation of God superior to that of any man since apostolic times.

The great Lutheran scholastic and theologian Johann Andreas Quenstedt also occupied himself with the question of Luther's call as a special divine intervention in the course of history. In Chapter XII, Question III, of his important work on *Systematic Theology,* the *Systema theologicum,* Quenstedt agreed with Gerhard's six proofs of the extraordinary divine appointment of Luther to reform the church, and offered additional proofs. Among these was Luther's restoration of the doctrine of justification and the evangelical doctrine of faith. Also the extraordinary efficacy of the reformer's prayers and the marvelous hymns which he produced were cited as further evidences and proofs that the living God was in and with Luther revealing himself to men.

At the same time, however, Quenstedt was much concerned to show that Luther's call was not extraordinary so as to undermine the legitimacy of his ministry and make him equal to the Zwickau prophets and other visionaries and sectarians who claimed extraordinary calls and special divine revelations. In Section Three of the twelfth chapter of his didactic and polemical theological work, the *Theologia didactico-polemica,* Quenstedt pointed out that Luther himself did not defend his authority as reformer by appeal to an immediate and extraordinary divine call. Rather he emphasized the official character of his office of priest and doctor of the church catholic, and the evangelical continuity of his action with everything that was truly apostolic and catholic in the church. This emphasis was necessitated by the severe criticism of the papal party which viewed any reference to Luther's extraordinary divine call to reform the church as a sure sign of ungodly and diabolical arrogance. In their anti-Roman polemics, therefore, Quenstedt, Luther, and other evangelical theologians avoided references to the special divine call of Luther. Söderblom stresses, however, that we today must focus our attention on both the ordinary and the extraordinary elements in Luther's divine calling if we are to understand fully the dynamics of Luther and the Reformation.

ECUMENICITY

Söderblom liked to view Martin Luther as the prototype of an evangelical catholic. Luther's was always an essentially ecumenical vision in which sectarian and schismatic tendencies have no abiding and rightful place. He was a devoted evangelical son of the church catholic to whom the thought of founding a separate order or institution or denomination in order to escape the corruption and abuses of the religious institution of his day was essentially alien. Deeply attached to the spiritual roots of the ecumenical church, he remained a loyal servant of the church catholic even after the Roman hierarchy of that day had expelled him.

The antiseparatist, antisectarian stance of Luther comes out clearly in his explanation of the meaning of the church in the Third Article of the Creed. No word is said about a visible against an invisible church, nor is separation urged between the sons of the Reformation and the Church of Rome. In his book on *Christian Fellowship,* Söderblom emphasizes the basically religious interpretation of the church universal which we find in Luther. The church is not primarily a sacred institution, but is called by the Spirit to forgiveness, peace, and hope through the Word of God. The focus of attention is the continued action of the living God and the Gospel through which the Spirit calls, gathers, enlightens, and sanctifies the flock of the Good Shepherd.

Söderblom believed that if Luther lived in this century, he would have a quite different view of the Vatican. Like the medieval Franciscan spiritualists, he got the impression that Rome was the seat of Satan and Antichrist. Nevertheless, Luther did not doubt that even in the Church of Rome the true Gospel was to be found, and this insight never left him, despite his mistaken notions regarding the real essence of the Roman papacy. His understanding of the church as the one holy Christendom helped him to avoid sectarian exclusiveness and complete blindness to truth, value, and meaning in other religious institutions. Söderblom notes with chagrin that the freedom and piety which enabled Luther to appreciate and preserve that which was of value in the Roman Church were notably absent in many of his disciples, so that Protestantism became greatly impoverished and depleted of catholic substance.

The church was for Luther both ecumenical and catholic. In his significant lecture entitled *Evangelic Catholicity,* Söderblom especially mentions the fact that Luther's explanation of the Third Article of the Creed is based on an understanding of the church as the whole of Christendom on earth. Thus Luther avoids the particularistic misunderstanding to which the word "church" was exposed already in Reformation times. At the same time he succeeds in bringing out more clearly the essential universality and catholicity of the church. Unfortunately the American text of the explanation of the Creed is based on the Latin text which reads *totam ecclesiam,* the whole church, rather than the original German which says, "die ganze Christenheit auf Erden," the whole Christendom on earth. Söderblom points out that the term "ecclesia," church, was rejected by Luther because the simple people might misunderstand it as a church building or it might be misunderstood as referring to the Roman Church, which at the time of the Reformation was the church. The literary and religious genius of Luther was not satisfied with anything less than the expression "one holy Christendom on earth" as the most accurate translation of the credal intention in the word "church."

It would be a mistake, however, to misunderstand Luther's ecumenical-mindedness as an expression of compromising laxity. His firm refusal to compromise the faith of the Reformation in order to satisfy the humanistic tendencies of the Swiss reformer Zwingli and thus achieve a pan-Protestant alliance against Rome is clear proof that, as Söderblom remarks in his perceptive essay on Luther in the light of ecumenicity *(Luther im Lichte der Ökumenizität),* for Luther the basis of Christian unity lay in the depths of Christian faith. Contemporary ecumenists can learn from Luther that clever compromises and happy phrases in the last analysis do not really unite Christians across denominational lines. The unity of the church is a matter of the depth dimension of Christian faith, divine revelation, and the personal experience of the power of the living God in the Christian community of faith. Ecumenism wells up in the hearts and minds of Christians who really love their Lord and God and who are truly committed members of his one holy evangelical and catholic church.

CHAPTER V

MISSION AND ECUMENISM

One of the characteristics of modern ecumenism has been the missionary vision of those committed members of the one holy evangelical and catholic church who pioneered the ecumenical reformation of twentieth-century Christianity. Söderblom had met many of the later leaders of the ecumenical movement at the meetings of the Student Christian Missionary Movement, and he himself had been a leader and literary spokesman for the Uppsala chapter of the Student Missionary Society. The meetings of missionary-minded students had inspired in him the serious interest in the history of religions which characterized his entire life.

Among the great historians of religion in the twentieth century Archbishop Nathan Söderblom occupies an important place. He was one of the first to recognize the decisive importance for Christianity and Christian missions of a new, realistic confrontation of the great religions of the world. An understanding encounter with non-Christian religions would, in his view, benefit the church in several ways.

THE BENEFITS OF ENCOUNTER

First, it would bring out more clearly the characteristic evangelical and catholic elements in Christianity. A comparison with other religions would disclose more fully the uniqueness of the Christian religion than would a comparison with the culture, its values, and its nonreligious isms. Thus the contemporary task of the Christian and the church can be clarified, and a more objective interpretation of the history of the church, its thought and practice, is made possible. Söderblom saw the need for such a reassessment arising especially out of the ecumenical movement. The striving for Christian unity would be continually frustrated and inhibited unless the history of the churches could be seen in a totally new light in which understanding and mutual appreciation and respect would replace polemics and misunderstanding, even misrepresentation, of historical facts.

Second, dialogues with Buddhism, Hinduism, Islam, etc., in their historical concreteness, enable the Christian to get the feel of what is essential to religion. In an age like ours when secularism and materialism threaten to undermine the foundations of Christian faith and life, a firm grasp of what constitutes the essence of religion is urgently needed. In the Christian perspective appropriate to an ecumenical age, the study of the history of the world's religions must therefore replace the concern with natural theology, Söderblom insisted, because the modern, scientific period, unlike earlier periods of history, has learned to understand nature without God.

Third, an objective attitude toward other religions will, according to Söderblom, provide the clue to the work of Christian missions in the future. In the twentieth century it is no longer possible to explain the remarkable similarities between Christianity and other religions as diabolical imitations produced by the devil in order to confuse the minds of the heathen and thus prevent their becoming Christians. This view of the universal presence of revelation may still have served the purpose of Jesuit missionaries in Latin America during the time of the Reformation, but today this explanation is no longer credible. But neither is it possible to be a responsible Christian missionary and ignore or push aside the fact that there exists a surprisingly large common ground between historically quite different religions. Söderblom pointed out that no religion is without revelation. The task of missionaries is therefore twofold: first, to recognize the presence and forms of this universal divine revelation and, second, to demonstrate convincingly that in Christianity, that is in Jesus Christ, is the most profound and enduring fulfillment of revelation.

Fourth, familiarity with non-Christian religions, and an objective study of their religious style and content, will in Söderblom's opinion lead to a relevant restatement of the function of miracles in religious life. The question of miracles continues to occupy the minds and emotions of both conservative and liberal Christians. Söderblom was convinced that this question was much more important for Christian faith than is commonly recognized today. He found that even such great theologians and Christians as Saints Augustine and Thomas Aquinas did not achieve a truly religious conception of miracles. Söderblom's constructive restatement of the traditional conception of miracle is most relevant today. The demythologizing theologian Rudolf Bultmann, the religionless Christianity of Dietrich Bonhoeffer, the God-is-dead theologians, the prophets of the secular city, the revelational positivist Karl Barth, and the ontological Paul Tillich are ultimately wrestling with the same problem. Tillich, for instance, insisted that Being was the key to the modern understanding of miracle. The miracle of miracles is that there is Being and not nothing. All other miracles are variations of the miracle of Being insofar as they are truly and factually miraculous, that is, revelatory of the power and ground of Being.

Fifth, Söderblom insisted that the missionary encounter with the reactivated living religions of the world today demanded the unified witness of all Christians. The way to achieve this unity was, and will be, according to Söderblom, the way of ecumenicity. In the twentieth century ecumenism is the requisite of Christian witness among non-Christians. Practically all of the younger churches are aware of this basic, inescapable necessity without which Christian growth and effective witness for Christ and his church are impossible on a large scale in the contemporary world. Fortunately a majority, but unfortunately not all, of the older churches are becoming aware that the ecumenical unity of all churches and Christians is not an optional luxury, but an inescapable necessity and sacred duty of the churches in the twentieth century.

THE UNIQUENESS OF CHRISTIANITY

For both the missionary and the ecumenical tasks of the churches, the clear and conscious awareness of what it is that constitutes the uniqueness of Christianity is, as Söderblom rightly insists, of great importance. The missionary effort of the churches can succeed only when the representatives of the Christian faith are themselves aware of the uniqueness of Christianity, that is, of that which distinguishes Christianity from all other religions. This uniqueness is what makes Christianity superior to all other religions. In many ways Christianity is continuous with the other religions of the world. Its unique elements are those points at which the Christian religion of revelation fulfills the dimly perceived aims and aspirations of all the religions of the world. Two things are therefore required of Christians in the modern world.

First, all must come to the full realization that "even pagans have known that 'we are also His offspring.' They have been 'feeling after Him.' And 'He has not let Himself be without witness.' We ought to read Origen's interpretation of such texts. It is high time in this age of world missions and world communications and the final flow of world history in one deep stream, that the Church acquaint itself with the thought of the general revelation of God."[1]

Second, in our ecumenical era we must be "attentive to the conditions of human association which have brought about a new order of things in our time," as the *Decree Concerning the Pastoral Office of Bishops in the Church,* promulgated at the Second Vatican Council, says so well. Ecumenical Archbishop Söderblom was acutely aware of this significant contemporary responsibility of Christianity, —a responsibility which for him extended beyond the churches to include also the non-Christian religions and isms of the world. The "new order of things in our time"[2] calls Christians everywhere to undertake a new, bold, and imaginative approach to non-Christians around the world. This approach must be based on concern and respect for the beliefs and practices of other religions and cultures. The respect here called for is ultimately grounded in the recognition that, while there is only one primary Old Testament, "there will be as many secondary Old Testaments to the one New Testament, as there are religions on the earth. Then we shall see that, strangely enough, Christ fulfills even the apostate lamentation ceremonies that, according to Hezekiah, eighth chapter, the women carried out with weeping and wailing for Tammuz at the temple of

Jerusalem, and that the Roman soldiers indicated an inner connection when they mockingly arrayed Pilate's Prisoner as a sort of spring king with a mantle and crown."[3]

GOD AS WILL

The concern for the uniqueness of Christianity permeates all of Söderblom's important writings. In his studies of non-Christian religions he discovered that one of the unique elements of biblical religion is its understanding of God as will. In his important book on *The Origins of Belief in God (Gudstrons uppkomst)*, he demonstrates that the religion of Moses is distinguished from other religions by its intense, personal awareness of the power of Yahweh, the God of Israel, and his inescapable, dynamic will. We find the ultimate basis for genuine biblical monotheism in the overwhelming awareness of the power of the God of Exodus and Sinai, rather than in philosophical speculation. The political, prophetic, and religious genius of Moses is the human agency through which the God of Abraham, Isaac, and Jacob reveals himself and thus makes an inescapable claim upon his people.

As a historian of religions Söderblom is fully aware of the continuity between the religion of Israel and the cults of the surrounding peoples. He recognizes that in the Old Testament the belief in an exalted, loving Shepherd of Israel and the mysterious, strong-willed Being of God, which is found in animism, have both been placed in the service of biblical revelation. The barbaric aspects of God's action in the lives and history of the Old Testament peoples may offend the aesthetic and moral sensibilities of enlightened, modern men. But Söderblom urges us to recognize that our knowledge of God and his will for us must always stand in a religious tension between the two poles of the God who can be known and the God who is incomprehensible. On the one hand, there is the reality of God as expressed in the Letter of Paul to the Romans: "Ever since the creation of the world his invisible nature, namely, his eternal power and deity, has been clearly perceived in the things that have been made" (Rom. 1:20). On the other hand, there is the mysterious, unpredictable, unknowable God: "How unsearchable are his judgments and how inscrutable his ways!" (Rom. 11:33b). "For my thoughts are not your thoughts, neither are your ways my ways, says the Lord" (Isa. 55:8). And yet there are not two Gods, the Known and the Unknown, but both have coalesced in biblical religion into the conception of the one Lord of Israel.

THE ANALOGY OF BEING

Söderblom's inquiries into the process of the genesis of our belief in God can make an important contribution to the contemporary problem of how men come to know God. Opposing solutions to the problem are vigorously put forth and hotly debated in our time. On the one hand, there are today's champions of the *analogia entis,* the analogy of being. They argue that from our knowledge of man and the world we can proceed to the knowledge of God by making certain inferences about the Being of God. There are analogies between our being and the nature of God, the Supreme Being. The radical God-is-dead theologians of contemporary Protestantism have followed the way of the *analogia entis,* the analogy of being, to its final conclusion. In their thinking the deity of God has become the divinity of Christ, and the divinity of Christ has become the humanity of Jesus. Language about God, let alone a transcendent God, has thus become meaningless. The business of the new, radical theologians is with the man Jesus of Nazareth, and not with deity or divinity. "The new essence of Christianity" (Hamilton) is "the secular meaning of the gospel" (Van Buren).

For the God-is-dead theologians there is nothing we can say as Christians about God that we cannot say about man. The analogy of being, the *analogia entis,* combined with an extreme form of nominalism that refuses to recognize as real any nonsecular and nonempirical Being, has led the new theologians of Protestantism to the point where they must declare the coming of age of secular man, and the death of God. In our time of the death of God emerges a new form of "godless Christology" (Hamilton), a doctrine of the person and work of Christ without God. All that really matters from now on is the man Jesus, who was the man for others.

THE ANALOGY OF FAITH

On the other hand, there are the protagonists of the analogy of faith, the *analogia fidei*. They denounce the *analogia entis* as an "invention of the Anti-Christ" (Karl Barth). These fideist theologians declare that the knowledge of the being of man and the world does not in fact lead us to the true knowledge of the God of the Bible but only to the God of whom the philosopher Ludwig Feuerbach said that he is man writ large. The one and only true God reveals himself in the Word of God, which became flesh in Jesus Christ. Apart from this self-revelation of God, which faith receives, there is no knowledge of God and no true knowledge of man. The *analogia fidei*, the analogy of faith, therefore proceeds from the concrete revelation of God at a particular time and place. Faith is the beginning of the knowledge and understanding of God.

The conception of God as will, which Söderblom developed and singled out as the unique conception of biblical religion, can help Christians out of the dilemma into which they are plunged by the mutually exclusive claims of the defenders of the analogy of being, on the one hand, and those of the analogy of faith, on the other. The primacy of the will in Christian discourse about God was first, and decisively, put forward by St. Augustine, and his thought has shaped and influenced the entire development of Christian life and thought from the close of the classical period to the present time. Söderblom makes connections with this basic insight of Western theology and relates it to the study of the religions of the world. According to him a comparison between biblical religion and other religions of the world shows that the two types of analogy, the *analogia entis* and the *analogia fidei*, are both necessary. Historically both have gone into the making of the God of Israel. In his early essay on *The Nature of Revelation*, Söderblom said already that if we had the eyes of God "all would lie clearly for us in its continuous process. In prophetic religion we cannot draw a line around certain words or certain events and say, here is God and revelation, there is man and nature. Even in the perfect revelation of God in the person of Christ, the divine and the human are commingled, as the theologians have expressed in the doctrine of the *communicatio idiomatum*."[4]

The ideas of God as process, and of history as continuous process, are fundamental presuppositions of Söderblomian thought. There are no static, fixed, and unchangeable meanings and realities of being or of faith. Reason and revelation, culture and faith, are at bottom characterized by process, change, and creative advance into novelty. The creative harmony and dynamic tension between the two interrelated ways of coming to know God, the way of the analogy of being and the way of the analogy of faith, must, according to Söderblom, continue throughout the process of Christian thought, because they correct and enhance one another to the greater glory of God among men in our time, as well as in the past and in the future.

THE TWO ANALOGIES IN BALANCE

Söderblom's understanding of the interdependence of the methods of the analogy of being and the analogy of faith can be of great value today in the areas of ecumenical and missionary endeavor. In the ecumenical movement it will help Christians to recover the biblical fullness of God, and to appreciate the ultimate unity of the Roman Catholic champions of the analogy of being and the Protestant protagonists of the analogy of faith. As in so many other ways, so here also, Protestant and Roman Catholic Christianity check, enhance, and correct one another. In the mission work of the churches the creative awareness of the unique interrelatedness of the analogies of being and faith in Christian religion can lead to a great, new, ecumenical breakthrough. The tremendous impact of the Barthian perspective on the younger churches, which are by reason of their relative lack of theological experience very vulnerable to the seductive fideism of Barthianism, only illustrates the great need for the kind of sane, balanced, dynamic, and progressive position which the ecumenical vision of Söderblom represents.

Archbishop Söderblom's concern for the uniqueness of Christianity and the integrity of the Christian proclamation in the twentieth century has been shared by many Christians across denominational lines. The ecumenical renewal of Christian awareness has led to a new emphasis on the church as a world missionary community. As the churches encounter the world's religions and isms in our rapidly changing and shrinking world, they are brought to a more profound realization of the essential character of the ecumenical church as a missionary reality.

In seeking to fulfill its destiny and to be true to its nature as a world-wide, evangelical, catholic, and orthodox Christian community, the church will be helped immensely by Söderblom's ecumenical vision of the interrelationship and continuity of religion and culture, faith and being, revelation and reason, *analogia fidei* and *analogia entis*. He never ceased to emphasize that the living God has revealed glimpses of his truth and being, of the nature and destiny of man, and of the meaning of life, in biblical as well as in non-Christian religions. The universal process of the gracious revelation of God includes all religions. Söderblom therefore looked forward to dialogues with Buddhists, Hindus, Moslems, and Jews with the same openness and sincerity and appreciative understanding with which he participated in whatever Protestant-Roman Catholic dialogue was possible during his lifetime. No religion is simply a product of culture, but all religions depend on the revelation of the living God which reason understands through faith. The all-encompassing process of religious revelation makes the knowledge of God, however dim, a universal, religious reality. But, Söderblom insists, only in the revelation of God in Jesus Christ can the human religious insights and longings for ideals of conduct, which have characterized the human quest for God throughout history, reach true fulfillment and achieve a universal, concrete, progressively changing, redemptive significance.

REVELATION IN HISTORY

One of the unique elements of biblical religion is its conception of "religion as revelation in history," as Söderblom calls it in his last great book, *The Living God.* He stresses there that much of the difficulty which modern men have with Christianity is due to the fact that Christianity anchors the reality of God in certain concrete and particular events in the history of a particular people. "History is a stumbling-block to reason. Why should not prophets and mystics appear in orderly succession, everywhere, in all civilizations? The attempt has been made to collocate the different religions so as to make a system, where one sets forth one side, and another another side of the spiritual equipment of man and his knowledge of God, and where, at the same time, progress from the lower to the higher can be discerned. But into systems of that kind, constructed by a Schleiermacher, a Hegel, and others, the history of religion cannot be squeezed."[5] Yet, strange as it may seem to us, in the confusing puzzle of history the God of Israel reveals himself. He shapes the history of his people and guides their ethical decisions. The uniqueness of biblical religion is that it does not seek God outside social and political reality in metaphysics, or in the infinity of the absolute One, but in history, because existence is at bottom history. God acts in particular and concrete events of history which then shape the destiny of the entire process of history and human existence. "The process and the end cannot be seen. For it is a process of creation. It contains an element of volition. Man is called to be the collaborator of the Creator. And *that* he is, not only the poet, the inventor, and the statesman, but every man who lives a spiritual and moral life."[6]

Söderblom's conception of history as process, and as the central framework of a uniquely Christian religious point of view, is an important contribution to the theological enterprise of the twentieth century. After the disillusionment with idealism there has been in our time a pronounced return to biblical and historical categories of Christian thought. A reflection of one phase of this movement is the successive quests of the historical Jesus which since Albert Schweitzer's epoch-making *Quest of the Historical Jesus* at the beginning of the century have agitated the minds of New Testament scholars and theologians. Söderblom's insights can be of great help in charting the course of the future of theology. He has continually emphasized that the historical character of Christian revelation and religion must not be interpreted so as to exclude philosophy and metaphysics altogether. For instance, he observes a remarkable and by no means merely accidental affinity between the process thought of the French philosopher Henri Bergson and the Weltanschauung, the world view, of the prophets of the Old Testament. This is particularly evident in the Bergsonian conception of *la durée,* the world-process.

More recently the Roman Catholic process theologian Teilhard de Chardin, building upon Bergsonian process categories, has sought to state the unique vision of the Christian religion in a way which substitutes the dynamic understanding of creative, evolutionary process for the old, static notion of fixed substance of classic Aristotelo-Thomism. Instead of relegating evolution or process to the accidental or phenomenal as opposed to the metaphysical or substantial, Teilhard shows that reality is process and process is evolution, in which the "substance" of a thing or person cannot be defined apart from its essential relatedness to the world. Every entity, spiritual or physical, is related in an evolving world which is essentially unfinished. In this kind of world "to stay put is to die. Permanency is falsehood; process is truth. The reason is that the domain of being and truth is the future, and the only way to attain the future is to be in time. To be outside time, then, is untruth; while to be in time is truth."[7] Time is, of course, the presupposition of history; without time there is no history. In the Teilhardian scheme there is thus a decidedly historical orientation in which the notion of being is "converted from being as substance to being as process; from being as an island, to being-with-another; for existence is a sharing, is a union."[8]

Some Protestant theologians have been attracted by the philosophy of organism developed by the process thinker Alfred North Whitehead, and have sought to answer Harvey Cox's call for a theology of dynamic process and rapid change. Cox himself called for the substitution of politics for history in theological discourse, because of the popular understanding that history deals with things that are past and about which nothing can really be done now. Of course, history in Söderblom's theology included the present and the future, so that what we mean by politics would constitute only a small part of the total responsibility of the churches in today's world. But Cox's basic intention aims at history as process with rapid social change and even revolution constituting the basic dynamisms in terms of which the Christian faith must be stated if it is to be applicable and relevant in the contemporary world. Thus far, however, the new theologians of Protestantism have not shown the care and circumspection which is characteristic of the Söderblomian treatment of the subject of revelation in history.

It is true that Teilhard and Whitehead combined the vision of universal process with a profoundly humanistic concern which was at the same time remarkably sensitive to the genuinely religious values and viewpoint. But whether we are Teilhardians or Whiteheadians or secular theologians, there is a great deal to learn from Söderblom's vision of ecumenicity. His biblical consciousness and his awareness of the concrete and irreducibly particular nature of the process of history form a unique harmony that is yet to be surpassed by a twentieth century theologian. In the years ahead he will remain an invaluable guide for the future of theology in general and ecumenical theology in particular.

THE PRINCIPLE OF PERSONALITY

In his significant treatise on *The Nature of Revelation* Söderblom points to the principle of personality as one of the unique marks of biblical religion and, within biblical religion, of evangelical Christianity. An objective comparison between the Christian religion and nonbiblical religions, and between various types of Christianity, shows that "the principle of personality is the strength of Evangelical Christianity. It knows only one authority, the authority of personality."[9] Söderblom is concerned to stress the uniqueness of Christianity in terms of the role which personality plays in its development. This uniqueness is bound up with the fact that in the Christian religion "revealed religion has reached its perfection, not in a perfect doctrine or guide to salvation, but in a person. 'For other foundation can no man lay than that which is laid, which is Jesus Christ.' In this person the Divine and human, the objective and the subjective are fused."[10] Genuine Christianity is thus what Söderblom, in *The Living God,* called "the religion of incarnation." To the question as to what it was that made Christianity something uniquely new, he answers: "The new thing was not a message, not a doctrine, but an historic person, *an actual man,* Jesus revealed as Christ and as the eternal Son originating a new life."[11]

For Söderblom religion divides itself into two basic types of mysticism or communion with God: the mysticism of infinity and the mysticism of personality. In some form or other the aim of every religion is communion with the divine. But some forms of religion seek this communion in terms of a mystical longing for absorption or mystical union with the Infinite; the soul is like a drop of water that returns to the eternal and infinite ocean of the divine. Other forms of religion enter into communion with the divine Life through personal communion after the manner of Jesus, Paul, and Martin Luther. In this evangelical form of personality-mysticism, as Söderblom calls it, the emphasis is on personality, will, dualism, and struggle. The book of 1910 on *The Religious Problem in Catholicism and Protestantism* transfers this typology into the area of religious symbolism and distinguishes between symbols derived from nature, e.g., the drop in the ocean, and symbols derived from human personality, e.g., the Father symbol of the Gospels. The former is a favorite with infinity mystics, the latter is most meaningful to personality mystics.

The contemporary significance of Söderblom's insight that the uniqueness of Christianity is intimately related to the process of personality can be illustrated by the development of related ideas in subsequent Roman Catholic, Orthodox, and Protestant thought. For instance, the Roman Catholic theologian Teilhard de Chardin, in his remarkable book on *The Phenomenon of Man*, develops the idea that the process of the universe is a collector, not primarily of energy, but of persons. We are living, according to Teilhard, in an irreversibly personalizing universe. The Omega point, to which the evolving universe is moving, is a spiritual center of persons at which the lines traversed by the evolution of man converge. This point leads into the pleroma, the fullness of the Christ of God.[12]

Orthodox theologians like Nicolas Berdyaev have developed the principle of personality more in correlation with the idea of *sobernost* community and communion than with that of evolution. Man enters the new life in Christ through the community of authentic persons. He becomes truly a person as he lives in authentic Christian communion with his fellow men. Genuine personhood is inseparable from the moral life; radical ethicality is of the essence of *Freedom and the Spirit* and of *The Destiny of Man.*

In Protestant theology the concern with the symbol of personality as central to Christianity's unique essence has been noticeable in many quarters. It is a dominant motif of the God-is-dead school of new Protestant theology, and some of its representatives (e.g., Altizer, to whom reference has been made in Chapter I) have explicitly acknowledged the illumination which Söderblom's insights into the centrality of human personality in the revelation of the Word of faith have brought them. Ideas akin to Söderblom's understanding of the principle of personality have been developed along existentialist lines by theologians like Rudolf Bultmann. In the Bultmannian scheme the uniqueness of Christian personality mysticism has become the "authentic existence" of the person liberated by Christ.

THE PROBLEM OF SUFFERING AND EVIL

Söderblom's study of history convinced him that a very important phase of the principle of personality is the creative affirmation of suffering. The uniqueness of Christianity is intimately connected with its positive evaluation of the inescapable fact of suffering. In his book on *The History of the Passion of Christ, Kristi pinas historia* (2nd ed., 1928), the theological focus of the Söderblomian perspective is specified in terms of Christ's vicarious suffering symbolized and epitomized by the mystery of the cross. All other religions, though they dimly feel toward the idea of redemption through suffering, fail to take the problem of suffering seriously, or they provide a quite unsatisfactory answer. Buddhism is the only religion, outside of Christianity, that deals with the problem of suffering. But its answer is negative: suffering is the spur that drives man to seek salvation in escape from the world and flight into the nothingness of Nirvana. The nearest approximation to the positive, vicarious evaluation of suffering in Christianity is the decision of the Buddha not to seek extinction in Nirvana, although he could have done so, but to stay on and endure suffering in order to proclaim the liberating *dhamma,* or way of salvation, and only after having accomplished this vicarious mission to dissolve in Nirvana nothingness. In Christianity, however, the central symbol of the faith is the cross, the symbol of vicarious suffering. From the cross Jesus Christ is calling all men, not to try to escape suffering, but to take it willingly upon themselves and thus to follow him.

As an ecumenical thinker, Söderblom devotes special attention to the unitive function of suffering. At the Stockholm ecumenical conference in 1925, Christians united by a common experience of suffering gathered around the Christian symbol of redemptive suffering, the cross of Christ, more relevant today than ever before. Ecumenical conferences and dialogues, as well as practical cooperation and united action are important in the Söderblomian vision of the churches' ecumenical mission in the world. But in the ongoing process of ecumenism "greater than action is suffering—not the lifeless suffering to which we submit, but living, voluntary suffering— both for him who suffers, and for him for whom the suffering is borne; the suffering possesses a still higher value than action. For suffering carries on and perfects action, after the hand has lost its strength. Suffering unites more than acts can do."[13]

The principle of unity through suffering applies not only to ecumenicity, but also to the Christian's personal and collective communion with God. In the Old Testament, for instance, "the author of the seventy-third Psalm clutched God, . . . clasped him in spite of affliction, even felt himself more intimately united with his God through suffering. External experiences became secondary, heaven, earth, and hell became secondary, in comparison with communion with God. The author of Job arrived also at a novel and humiliating conception of the impudence and insufficiency of human thought, and bowed down in the dust before the inscrutable majesty of God. Now on Golgotha this prophecy was fulfilled. The usual explanation, due to causal law and general experience, became bankrupt."[14] Thus, Söderblom believes, "the cross became God's method for proving his love, which did not shrink back from anything, but recklessly used the most effective means."[15]

At this point Söderblom raises the important question: "How are we to explain the fact that Christianity, generally considered as the highest religion, introduces the hideous spectacle of the cross, abhor-

rent to every civilized taste?" And he answers: "I think that the
answer is obvious. Men had been seeking for God. The cross is the
strongest testimony that *God has been seeking man.* God's way is as
non-human as possible. But it is no mere idea; it is an historic fact
which has proved to be stronger than any other fact or conception
in religion. We must acknowledge the truth of St. Paul's observation: 'Because the foolishness of God is wiser than men.' God grasped
at humanity in order to lift it to his fatherly bosom. His hand was
grievously wounded, but he succeeded."[16]

Söderblom's answer raises a decisive question which strikes at the
very essence of the uniqueness of Christianity: Does God suffer? He
seems to answer this question in the affirmative, but his Yes is not
unambiguous. If God's "hand" was wounded—Söderblom is here perhaps referring to St. Irenaeus' famous simile of Christ and the Holy
Spirit as the two hands of God—does this mean that cruel suffering
lacerated the very bosom of the Father and tormented with terrible
wounds and pains the heart of God, his essence and innermost
nature? Or are we to make a distinction between God's "hand" and
God as he really is?

In practically all of Söderblom's great works the question of divine
suffering reoccurs in one form or another. The unique essence of
Christianity is, for him, inseparably related to the question of suffering. From the early essay on *The Nature of Revelation* (1903)
through the ecumenical theology of his *Christian Fellowship* (1923)
to his last great work on *The Living God* (1931) he wavers between
a clear endorsement of the idea that God himself (and not just his
"hand") suffers and the old, traditional notion of the impassibility
of God, according to which God, by definition, cannot suffer. On the
one hand, he is convinced that "God suffers. May one venture to
state: God Himself suffers? Is it not a heathen idea? Paganism knows
how to relate with ceremonies and words: a god, the god of life,
the saviour-god who suffers and dies, arising again to a new life.
For paganism the idea of a god's suffering is easier because it knows
many gods. Some of them may reign in blessed peace while another
god suffers. For Christianity, as for all monotheism, it is difficult.
There seems to be a contradiction. History and revelation show us
how Christ, God's supreme Son, the real Revealer, suffers and dies.

Dogmatics, that are more well-meaning and eager than Biblical and sound, have emphasized the divinity of Christ in a metaphysical way which incurs the risk of crucifying God the Father and of transforming Golgotha and Jesus' cry of anguish, *Eli Eli*, to a sort of sham manoeuvre in divinity."[17]

On the other hand, Söderblom realizes that "the Christian Church has always rejected the conclusion from the dogma of the divinity of Christ, that God Himself, the one, sole Almighty, suffers. But still this idea comes forth again in new forms, although it was already rejected by the Church in the so-called gnostic systems. How can we really believe and experience the living God in history and human life without imagining Him as suffering, when life and history are so full of suffering, or, more correctly, when what is new, significant, and blessed in history seems to be incapable of realization except through pain and death? Pascal saw the exalted Saviour still suffering in pangs of the Cross in heaven."[18] Torn between two aspects of the process of the reality of God he returns to the question: "Does God suffer with us and for us? And the answer has come, Yes. Amid strife and pain God realizes Himself and His dominion over the insensible order of nature and the resistance of evil and sloth. It is a troublesome and painful path. But if we obey the voice in our soul we have no choice. We must surrender to God in unconditional submission. We must ally ourselves with Him, take part in His struggle and pain, and, through the hindrances of nature, distress, and sin within us and without, be helped on by Him to His kingdom."[19]

But immediately the evangelical consciousness of the great catholic ecumenical theologian Söderblom speaks to him to remind him that "such an idea is incompatible with the First Article of our Confession of Faith. But it has deep roots in religious aspiration and in the Gospel. That is why the sacrifice of the Mass is so powerful and attractive, in spite of its incompatibility with our Lord's teaching. It is difficult to give up the pagan idea of a sacrificial priest. With the priest is connected the sacrifice. When it became impossible to sacrifice animals, the idea was developed, contrary to the Epistle to the Hebrews and the whole New Testament, of bloodlessly repeating Jesus' sacrificial death. It is not a Christian idea. But why has the sacrifice of the Mass such power? Why does it attract so many, even outside Roman Catholicism? The answer is obvious: There is a religious idea behind it. God has a share in our suffering."[20] Söderblom proposes a preliminary, tentative answer when he says that "a groping and dizzying conception of God Himself as suffering and struggling in the development of the world seems to me to come nearer to the strange, nay, tragic, conditions of this existence and the essence of Christianity than a view that arranges both God and the course of the world in a perfect harmony, where everything fits in splendidly from beginning to end. It may be a pity that we were not there to arrange the course of the world, but, as it is now, God's path must be through suffering, as must that of His congregation."[21]

Ideas akin to Söderblom's basic insight into the unique essence of Christianity as inseparably related to the reality of suffering in the development, or process, of the world have been receiving a remarkable amount of attention in contemporary theology. For instance, the new theologian William Hamilton has focused his attention on "Jesus as suffering Lord" in trying to spell out *The New Essence of Christianity*. Secular man, having lost a real sense of the transcendence of God, can today speak honestly and relevantly only of Christ's "Lordship as humiliation."

Related emphases are being made by recent theologians behind the iron curtain, too. For example, the East German theologian Hanfried Müller finds them to be most relevant to the contemporary situation of the church in a Marxist land. In his sensational book *From the Church to the World (Von der Kirche zur Welt*, Leipzig, 1961), Müller develops along Bonhoefferian lines certain ideas closely related to those of Söderblom about the suffering of God. The mystery of God is "the hiddenness of God in his suffering" (p. 395). The secret of the lordship and the mystery of the messiahship of Jesus is "that He who suffers in the world is the Lord of the world" (p. 396). Müller insists that "this secret must be guarded in order to protect the ultimate from being profaned, as well as in order to protect the penultimate from a premature judgment. The surrender of the Messianic secret would destroy the penultimate by pre-empting the judgment, the world would encounter the claim to power of a ruling church, instead of the witness of a suffering church. But thereby the ultimate, the Gospel, would be destroyed at the same time, it would have to become law . . . . The giving up of the Messianic secret, the renunciation of its content, would expose church and world to cheap grace" (pp. 396-397).

Söderblom's treatment of the significance of suffering for the right understanding of the uniqueness and essence of Christianity distinguishes itself from more recent developments of this topic by its greater concern for the whole Gospel, the fullness of Christian truth. As a truly ecumenical theologian he is always conscientiously faithful to the evangelical and catholic and orthodox breadth and height and depth of the faith and life of the church. Deeply suspicious of any monistic systematization of Christianity, he denounces every attempt to reduce the Christian religion to any one denominator or numerator as a rationalistic *tour de force* fashionable with men whose *Weltanschauung* harks back to cognates of the philosophies of the enlightenment or idealism. A biblical and genuinely Christian world view, according to Söderblom, is dualistic—not in the gnostic sense of a metaphysical dualism between matter and spirit, but in the ethico-religious sense of personal struggle against opposing forces as we find it in the prophets of the Old Testament, and in Jesus and his apostles. This Christian dualism is essential to the uniqueness of the Christian faith and must not be surrendered or watered down in ecumenical dialogue or in the Christian encounter with the religions of the world.

NOTES

1. Söderblom, *The Nature of Revelation,* pp. 10-11.
2. Second Vatican Council, *Decree Concerning the Pastoral Office of Bishops in the Church* (Huntington, Ind.: Our Sunday Visitor, Inc., 1965), p. 3b.
3. Söderblom, *Christian Fellowship,* p. 144.
4. Söderblom, *The Nature of Revelation,* p. 34.
5. Söderblom, *The Living God,* p. 264.
6 *Ibid.,* p. 314.
7. E. R. Baltazar, "Teilhard de Chardin: A Philosophy of Procession," *New Theology No. 2,* ed. Martin E. Marty and Dean G. Peerman (New York: Macmillan Co., 1965), p. 146.

8. *Ibid.*, p. 141.
9. Söderblom, *The Nature of Revelation*, p. 81.
10. *Ibid.*
11. Söderblom, *The Living God*, p. 321.
12. Pierre Teilhard de Chardin, *The Phenomenon of Man*, trans. Bernhard Wall, with introduction by Julian Huxley (New York: Harper & Row, 2nd edition 1965). Copyright © 1959 by Harper & Row, Publishers, Inc. Reprinted by permission.
13. Söderblom, *The Living God*, p. 343.
14. *Ibid.*, p. 341.
15. *Ibid.*, p. 342.
16. *Ibid.*, p. 344.
17. Söderblom, *Christian Fellowship*, p. 146.
18. *Ibid.*, pp. 146-147.
19. *Ibid.*, p. 147
20. *Ibid.*, pp. 147-148.
21. *Ibid.*, p. 148.

CHAPTER VI

THE CHURCH AND THE CHURCHES

The outreach of Christian missions is spiritually the work of the one holy catholic and apostolic church. However, because of the divisions that have split the visible image of the church in the world, the God-given unity of the church (a unity in the Spirit, as Söderblom always emphasized) is not discernible to the eyes of all men. Denominational divisiveness and missionary rivalries among the churches are, therefore, inhibiting or frustrating the unique mission of Christianity in the context of the religions of the world. Moreover, according to Söderblom, the stress on what divides one church from the others, and the ever-present need to explain to non-Christians why there are differences which make it impossible for Christian churches to work together in brotherly harmony, tend to obscure the uniqueness of Christianity. Hence Christian unity and cooperation must be recognized as a basic requirement of effective missionary work in the modern world—a belief which historically and theologically has stimulated the ecumenical movement for Christian unity.

In his book *Christian Fellowship or the United Life and Work of Christendom*, Archbishop Söderblom outlines three methods of promoting Christian unity. These methods indicate practical and concrete ways in which the churches can be brought closer together in spirit and in action. Their ultimate aim is to bridge as much as possible the gap between the credo which declares the faith in one holy catholic and apostolic church, and the contemporary reality of Christian disunity and division into hundreds of sects, churches, and denominations. The fact that today it is fashionable to engage in dialogue with the separated brethren behind the walls of other denominational structures is a hopeful sign of the possibility of remedying this situation in the future, but it does not decisively alter the present dilemma of the one church and the many churches.

One method of promoting Christian unity is that of absorption. The answer to the problem of the relationship between the one church of faith and the many contemporary denominations and churches is here given in terms of institutional absorption of the many into one. Traditionally, the chief protagonist of this method has been the Roman Catholic Church. The exclusivism of Roman Catholicism prior to Vatican II has rendered this method unacceptable to all non-Roman denominations. Developments during and since the Second Vatican Council have indicated that major modifications of this view are in the process of emergence. Söderblom's principal objection to the institutional method is that it "leaves no room for the other spiritual homes of Christendom" (p. 122). He is not opposed to institutional unity as such. As a churchman and archbishop he realizes that the institutional principle is of great value to the church's growth, survival, and expansion. But he is against an institutionalism that undermines the spirit of the Gospel and does violence to the freedom of Christians in their contemporary political, cultural, and historical concreteness.

The dynamics of the Christian Gospel and the form of Christian unity stand in creative tension in Söderblom's conception of how the churches can be reconciled to one another. The Söderblomian dialectic of dynamics and form continues to be relevant in the World Council of Churches and the Roman Catholic Church since Pope John XXIII. Coming from opposite poles—the World Council of Churches starting with a strong emphasis on ecumenical dynamics and moving toward viable structures, the Roman Catholic Church of Vatican II coming from a traditional concern for form and moving toward dynamic, ecumenical freedom—both are beginning to converge on a common ground of ecumenicity. Söderblom's recognition of the continued necessity of a wholesome tension between Christian dynamics and form in the ecumenical movement can provide a most valuable guideline for future ecumenical progress. His ecumenical vision can help the churches steer a wise middle course between the right-wing Roman Catholic Scylla of authoritarian institutionalism and the left-wing Protestant Charybdis of denominational chaos.

Another of the three ways of uniting presently separated Christians is what Söderblom terms the method of faith. Christian unity can, according to this view, be realized without abolishing all of the presently existing denominations. The Holy Spirit is the true creator of ecumenical communion between Christians everywhere. As the Spirit of God calls Christians in every denomination to repentance through the Word of God, the foundations of ecumenicity are being laid. The Spirit and the Word of God must continually chasten the churches, in order that Christians in each one of the separated churches may increase in faith, progress in hope, and grow in love. Thus the grace of the Holy Spirit is at work through the method of faith. The result of its activity is that—as the Vatican *Decree on Ecumenism* says so well, in profound harmony with Söderblom's basic, ecumenical vision—"there increases from day to day a movement, fostered by the grace of the Holy Spirit, for the restoration of unity among all Christians."[1]

For Söderblom, ecumenical faith is always active in the love of duty and the hope of the promises of God in Christ. Christian unity in the fundamentals of Christian faith "is inseparable from our duty as Christians and it belongs to our Saviour's promise."[2] This promise, which is the basis of the ecumenical faith of the churches, is bound up with the coming of the Holy Spirit. "When the Spirit of truth comes, he will guide you into all the truth" (John 16:13). Söderblom sees a concrete evidence of the promise of the Spirit in the work of the ecumenical Faith and Order movement devoted to the promotion of Christian understanding in the areas of doctrine and church organization. He recognizes its importance for the future progress of ecumenicity even though he himself is more involved in the ecumenical Life and Work movement with its concerns for practical Christianity and interdenominational cooperation.

In Söderblom's view, the understanding of faith as a basis for Christian unity must be broadened and deepened if it is to serve as an effective agent in promoting ecumenism. He is confident that if this broadening and deepening are carried out with a view toward its contemporary relevance, it will show that "three great problems—the enigma of suffering love and expiation, the craving for the absolute and unconditioned in religion, and the faith in unity—are lessons taught by God without difference of confessions and Church organizations.[3] The existence of serious divisions and opposing creeds in contemporary Christianity indicates that "creeds and venerable formulas are not sufficient for the settling of our problem, but that Christian thought is bound to dive afresh into the depths of actual experiences in order to find a unity that formulas and external divisions may conceal."[4]

The contemporary importance of this insight is recognized by the World Council of Churches as well as by the Roman Catholic Church. For example, the *Decree on Ecumenism* of the Second Vatican Council declares that it is ecumenically both necessary and desirable that Christians in every denomination should engage in "ecumenical dialogue"—"with love for the truth, with charity, and with humility,"[5] in order to penetrate more deeply into the depths of actual experiences of human and divine realities and mysteries. If the ecumenists engaging in dialogue are loyal to the truth of the Christian faith, "this kind of 'fraternal rivalry' will incite all to a deeper realization and a clearer expression of the unfathomable riches of Christ"[6] Christians everywhere are thus brought closer together as they meet the common challenge of giving a relevant expression of the faith of the churches, a faith which despite its apparent disharmony is at bottom the one faith in the one Lord of all.

A third way to Christian unity is what Söderblom calls "the method of love." In the early stage of the ecumenical movement (and we have presently just barely begun to enter this stage) practical Christian cooperation holds out the greatest promise of getting the ecumenical movement off the ground. Its pragmatic nature makes it possible for Christians to join together in common ecumenical tasks, even though they are still separated by different dogmas and conceptions of the ministry. The method of love enables Christians from widely differing denominations to unite in a common concern and action for the care of the contemporary world. Söderblom insistently reminds his fellow Christians in the twentieth century that "our own work in His service as well as the distress of our generation renders systematic co-operation imperative. Otherwise we are in danger of wasting noble strength and experiencing the bitterness of unnecessary failure—unnecessary because the lack of confidence and clear, mutual understanding, free from vain confusion and unseemly interference, produces unnecessary weakness."[7]

Later developments in the ecumenical movement have amply vindicated the wisdom of Söderblom's ecumenical vision. Not only did the practical Christianity of the Life and Work movement achieve the first great ecumenical gathering of twentieth-century ecumenicity under Söderblom's leadership, but his method, with the necessary modifications which historical change demands, has continued to be one of the most fruitful avenues of Christian understanding and relevant ecumenism. The method of love, however, must not be separated from the method of faith, or be opposed to it. These two methods complement one another. In the final structure of ecumenical process, as envisioned by Söderblom, they must interpenetrate one another and be united in a dynamic' ecumenical harmony which will unite the churches in freedom. The dimensions of the structure of Söderblomian ecumenicity may be set forth under twelve heads.

1. Orthodoxy

The ecumenical dictum attributed to Archbishop Söderblom, according to which "doctrine divides but service unites," is sometimes misunderstood as an expression of his alleged indifference or hostility toward the truth of Christian faith. Söderblom did use this phrase —which, incidentally, he claimed he first learned from the German Lutheran theologian and churchman Kappler at the constituting convention of the Lutheran World Convention at Eisenach, Germany, in 1921—mainly in order to indicate that all Christians can cooperate right now in common, practical concerns. This ecumenical cooperation would tend to make the churches a more effective witness for Christ in the world of today.

At the same time, Söderblom was fully aware that the fullness of ecumenicity demanded a genuine concern for *orthodoxa*, that is, for right doctrine and—as his ecumenical friend, the Orthodox theologian Nicolas Glubokowsky reminded him—right praise. In Söderblom's conception of the ecumenical trinity of evangelicity, catholicity, and orthodoxy, the question of the truth which will make

Christians free was of decisive significance. All Christians are called by the Holy Spirit through the Word of God to participate actively in the ecumenical movement. In the context of this movement "sacred and great is our task to learn from one another, to be taught by the Spirit through each other, in order finally to become of one mind, not only in love, but also in the doctrinal expressions for the revealed truth, and to sit all together at our Saviour's feet, listening to His voice with burning hearts."[8] The ecumenical vision of the churches' movement toward unity is inconceivable for Söderblom without orthodoxy. Christian ecumenicity and unity is an inescapable and most urgent necessity, but it must be promoted in obedience to the Spirit of truth. The essence of ecumenism is thus bound up with orthodoxy and its concern for the fullness of truth.

The history and development of the ecumenical movement in both Roman Catholicism and the World Council of Churches illustrate the continued relevance of the Söderblomian insistence on a high, sober, and balanced regard for Christian truth and right doctrine. No lasting and worthy ecumenical unity can be achieved at the price of truth. The unity of the churches must be a unity in truth as well as in deed. In Söderblom's ecumenical vision this concern was united with an active pragmatism which added flexibility and realism to his concern for the faith of the church. The harmony of these two major emphases of ecumenism is a continuing challenge to the churches as they move closer together in the ecumenical stream.

2. Intercommunion

When he was still a theological professor at the University of Uppsala, Söderblom had already stimulated interest in closer ties with the Church of England. He pointed out that for a Lutheran theologian and churchman there was a good deal worth learning from the history, the life, and the thought of Anglicanism. Furthermore, he welcomed and followed up on the suggestion made at the Lambeth Conference of 1888 and 1897 that the Church of Sweden, with its unbroken apostolic succession, offered possibilities for close cooperation with the Church of England. When, before the Lambeth Conference of 1908, inquiries were made with Archbishop Ekman of Sweden about closer ties between the two churches, Söderblom encouraged the commencement and continuation of negotiations between the two parties. Thanks largely to the far-sighted and creative persistence of Söderblom's efforts at the conference table and through publications the negotiations were successful. In 1922, after fourteen years of effort, and in Söderblom's eighth year as Swedish Primate, intercommunion between the Church of England and the Church of Sweden was authorized by both sides.

The establishment of intercommunion between churches meant for Söderblom that a small but concrete victory had been won in the ecumenical campaign of the churches for reunion as one church. The ecumenical significance of intercommunion varies, depending on the nature of the communions involved. Söderblom, for example, saw the establishment of intercommunion between Anglicanism and Swedish Lutheranism as the building of a bridge between Anglicanism and Protestantism. This ecumenical bridge, of which the archdiocese of Uppsala formed the center under Söderblom's dynamic world leadership, provided a common meeting ground for Protestantism, Anglicanism, and Eastern Orthodoxy.

3. Renewal

Archbishop Söderblom insisted that the practice of ecumenism must involve a renewal of the church through an increased fidelity to its own calling. He did everything in his power to renew the life of the Church of Sweden. Many deserted village churches were renovated and reopened. Efforts were made to incorporate into the Swedish hymnal the songs of the evangelical revival, many of which were dear to the people. Söderblom himself had a profound appreciation for the devotional power and warmth of these spiritual folksongs, and he endeavored to use them for the enrichment of the worship of the church.

The revival of biblical and relevant preaching was closely connected with Söderblom's enhancement of the hymnody of the church. For him Bible and hymnbook belonged together. Already in his early book on *Jesus' Sermon on the Mount and Our Time* (1898) he emphasized that the biblical ideals presented in the Sermon on the

Mount are not just prudent rules for successful daily living, but revolutionary ideals which call us to social and moral repentance. In his later years this socio-ethical emphasis was enriched by his ecumenical concern for Christian unity. It amalgamated into the call for a new creed of the churches: practical Christian social action and ethical relevance, brotherly love, Christian unity, the brotherhood of all men, and world peace. These noble ideals Söderblom viewed as concrete, contemporary manifestations of that spiritual urge to perfection which is one of the portals of divine revelation and an essential element in every genuine religion. This urge has generally been a powerful factor in the occurrence of interior conversion, and without this conversion there was, for Söderblom, no ecumenicity worthy of the name.

4. Liturgical Recovery

The recovery of the liturgical treasures of the Swedish Church was one of the most controversial efforts of the Archbishop. He was continually criticized for the ecclesiastical protocol and ceremony which he displayed while in office. The low church men in Sweden and abroad were frightened by these catholicizing tendencies in the evangelical camp. And when Söderblom, in 1922, five years after the Bolshevik revolution, went over to Latvia and Estonia and consecrated the Lutheran superintendent there as archbishop, some low church Lutherans were terrified by the spread of Söderblomian "crypto-papism" abroad. But Söderblom did not yield to his low church critics at home and abroad. Rather he reminded them that the church has a catholic tradition of many centuries which seeks to give a dignified form to the worship and actions of the church. To reject this great and valuable tradition would be a deplorable one-sidedness and would fail to do justice to the genuine value of ancient tradition and dignified style which is part of the catholic dimension of Christianity.

From his studies in the history of religions Söderblom had learned that religion is drama. He brought out and wore the ancient and symbolic liturgical vestments which had been preserved from the Middle Ages through the Reformation to the present time. He loved to chant the solemn high mass, and to play and hear the great music of the church. He believed firmly that the revelation of God could be effectively mediated through music and art. "If I were asked for a fifth Gospel," he once said, "I should not hesitate to name the interpretations of the secret of the redemption that reached its climax in Johann Sebastian Bach."[9] Revelation was for Söderblom a continuous process of God's judgment and redemption in history, which could be made visible and audible for the believers in worship.

5. The Saints

Archbishop Söderblom sought to recover a meaningful concept of sainthood. The evangelical concept of a saint was to him part of his ecumenical vision. The status of a saint was in his opinion bound up with the question of revelation. Did, or does, this person reveal in his life and being the living God? That was the decisive question which determined whether someone was a true saint or not. Archbishop Söderblom and Pope John XXIII would, under this definition of sainthood, deserve to be canonized as saints of the ecumenical church.

In his lecture of 1925, entitled "The Evangelical Concept of a Saint," Söderblom distinguished between worldly deeds and saintly deeds. In the former case we are dealing with great and good deeds which men do and which result in the praise of the deeds done, or in the glorification of the men who did them. In the latter case we are confronted with great and good deeds which cause us to glorify God rather than praise men. The character of these latter thoughts, words, and deeds is such that their praise cannot remain with men on earth, but must rise to God in heaven. Actions like these are performed by those who are saints in the true sense of the word. They disclose the power of the living God by what they are, and say, and do.

Söderblom stressed the universality and continuity of the process of revelation, in the church and the world, through saints and creative genius. He felt himself part of the catholic communion of saints. On the day which marked the anniversary of the death of St. Eric of Sweden it was Söderblom's custom to go to the Cathedral of Uppsala and to pray at that saint's relics. The same he did on the anniversary day of the death of the Swedish reformer and archbishop Laurentius Petri, and other great saints of Christianity and the Church of Sweden. Thus Söderblom exhibited his unique ability to combine profound, evangelical piety with a catholic appreciation for the great history and tradition of the whole church. His tendency was to give preference to the saints who actively stood and fought in the midst of human life over those saints who sought to cultivate their own holiness by ascetic exercises and seclusion.

6. Social Concern

The first four years of Söderblom's career as archbishop were filled with the terror of World War I. Although safe in neutral Sweden, he suffered greatly under the fact that the divided churches stood powerlessly by while the madness of destruction raged in Europe and other parts of the world. At the same time the class struggle, led by militant, antichurch socialists and atheistic communists, threatened to engulf many of the nations of Europe. Thus the social concerns of the Life and Work movement, under the leadership of Söderblom, received a tremendous impetus through the war and the social unrest of the times. The archbishop was also interested in the Faith and Order movement and its concern with doctrinal and liturgical matters and differences, a movement which had grown out of the Edinburgh Conference of 1910 and was led by Bishop Charles Brent of the Protestant Episcopal Church in the U.S.A. Söderblom's primary concern, however, was the social, moral, and ecumenical thrust of the Life and Work movement. This concern reached its first great climax in the Stockholm Conference of 1925, when Anglicans, Protestants, and Orthodox religious leaders ranging from patriarch to archbishop, bishop, and elder met in one of the most impressive gatherings of the ecumenical movement in the twentieth century.

The movement accepted the churches as they were and did not attempt to adjust their theologies or reconcile their different concepts of what constitutes a valid ministry. Driven on by the ecumenical vision of the church catholic, Söderblom wanted the different churches to demonstrate that the Christian faith transcends the divisions between races, classes, and nations in the direction of one, universal, united Christendom. By Christendom Söderblom meant the contemporary reality of the church in its multiphasic scope of evangelical, catholic, and orthodox branches. The characteristically sectarian abhorrence for the concept of Christendom was not shared by the great evangelical catholic Nathan Söderblom. Despite great obstacles and delays, he helped to bring together the ecumenical Stockholm Conference in order to demonstrate in concrete and living form the scope of Christian unity. Unfortunately, the Roman Catholics refused Söderblom's invitation to send one or more representatives or observers to this ecumenical conference on Life and Work.

7. World Peace

Closely related to Söderblom's concern for universal, Christian cooperation in matters of a social and moral nature was his active promotion of world peace. He considered the work for peace part of his duty as Primate of the Church of Sweden, and hoped that the spirit of ecumenicity would create a new atmosphere of international understanding and good will among churches and Christians everywhere. The practice of ecumenism and the search for peace on earth have continued to be closely related to this day. The courageous and timely calls to peace which the ecumenical Popes Paul and John XXIII have so urgently issued are evidences of the inseparability of ecumenism and world peace.

In 1930 Nathan Söderblom was awarded the Nobel Peace Prize. Thus the secular world also gave special recognition to the archbishop's ecumenical quest for universal peace through Christian unity.

8. The Catholic Vision

Archbishop Söderblom's catholic vision could not be obstructed by doctrinal or denominational divisiveness. Many of the differences which one generation might view as irreconcilable appear in a quite different light when placed in the broader perspective of the catholic history and tradition of the whole church. "Short-sighted eyes see only the differences," he once remarked. "Distance teaches us a useful lesson. In the cathedral close to my window, beside the relics of the beloved king and patron saint of Sweden, St. Eric, men are buried who considered veneration of saints a dangerous thing. Medieval prelates, until Archbishop Jacob Ulfson and others, who considered the beginning of the Reformation the ruin of religion, repose there peacefully with King Gustavus Vasa, who adopted the Reformation for the realm, and likewise his great Archbishop Laurentius Petri, our Church Father, who devoted a long life to introduce the evangelical spirit into the church and the nation. King John III, the learned, Erasmian believer, his noble, Roman Catholic, Polish queen, and Emanuel Swedenborg, the revealer of a new dispensation, have found their last place of rest with the sturdy, Lutheran prelates who thundered against them from the pulpit of the cathedral."[10]

The silent protest against a false kind of exclusiveness which the great dead resting in many of the famous sanctuaries of Christendom make strengthened Söderblom's conviction that the only sure foundation of the great ecumenical church of the future is evangelical catholicity. His catholic vision was inclusive rather than exclusive. It included great Christians of all ages and of various persuasions. It lived in and with the catholic tradition of the Church of Sweden and the whole church of Christ on earth. He deplored the vague and inadequate conceptions of the one holy catholic church which rationalism and the pietistic revival had introduced into Sweden and the rest of the Protestant world. These notions of the one holy church fall short of the true reality of the church in its universality and completeness. For Söderblom the church was the one, invisible body of Christ which is revealed in his flock on earth.

9. Evangelicity

In addition to his catholic vision, Archbishop Söderblom was unequivocally committed to the genuine spirit of evangelicity. The essence of this spirit was for him "an overwhelming sense of the greatness of God's free grace as granting forgiveness and peace to the troubled human heart and saving men from perdition, not through their own perishable endeavors and observances and works, but through faith in Jesus Christ."[11] Evangelicity means joy in the grace and forgiveness of God which brings peace through the Gospel. Without the gracious forgiveness of Christ, the troubled human heart and conscience finds no rest. It seeks to justify itself by means of its achievements, but fails continually and thus falls ever deeper into spiritual misery and bondage.

A further characteristic of Söderblomian evangelicity is the central place which the Gospel occupies as the revelation of God in Christ. The Gospel is the good news which Jesus Christ seeks to bring to the world. It is the Gospel of God's grace in Christ which frees us from the law of death. The central principle of the Gospel is that of faith and love which, under the guidance of the Holy Spirit, can be applied freely to every human condition.

Finally, Söderblom insisted, evangelicity means freedom, the freedom for which Christ has set us free. It involves freedom from the oppression of biblicism, fundamentalism, superstition, moralism, work-righteousness, and ecclesiastical authoritarianism. With particular reference to the Church of Sweden, Söderblom pointed to two enemies of evangelical freedom.

The one enemy seized upon certain ceremonies, customs, and vestments, which were all either indifferent or opposed to the true Gospel, and claimed that they were necessary for salvation. Although most characteristic of the degeneration of Christianity during the later Middle Ages, this enemy of Christian freedom is not completely vanished even today.

The other enemy of evangelical freedom threatens the church and Christianity from the other side by pretending that the destruction of time-honored traditions, venerable customs, beautiful and artistic Christian ornaments, and dignified vestments is an essential requisite for salvation, even though they are not contrary to the Gospel, but simply *adiaphora* with respect to the essence of Christian faith. Despite the fact that they are in themselves irrelevant to the substance of the Gospel, evangelical Christian freedom must consider many of them dear to faithful people of the church. For Archbishop Söderblom the respect and reverence for vestments, ceremonies, and customs which have become dear to the generations and are not opposed to the pure evangelical message of the Gospel, is a sign of genuine, evangelical freedom.

The classic expression of evangelicity Söderblom found in Martin Luther and his *Small Catechism.* It is classic because of its timeless value, truth, and relevance. The *Small Catechism* is a positive statement of evangelical Christianity in simple yet profound form. Although written when Luther was at the height of his struggle against the nominalist perversion of medieval Christianity and the papacy, the *Small Catechism* remains completely free of odious polemics. In his book on Luther's *Small Catechism,* Söderblom extolled it as both the literary masterpiece of the greatest religious genius since Paul and the most popular of all of Luther's evangelical writings. The archbishop closed his book on the *Catechism* in a manner which is rather typical of his evangelical stance. He wrote: "Shortly after its appearance, the *Catechism* happened to fall into the hands of a high Roman prelate, who did not know who the author was. He exclaimed: 'Blessed is the hand that has written this book.' I say: Blessed is he who can live through the ups and downs of life, and in his last hour still make the confession of his catechism: Jesus Christ is my Lord."[12]

10. The Cross

The cross of Christ was the center of the ecumenical theology of Archbishop Nathan Söderblom. The reasons for his view were chiefly three. First, the cross was for him a mystery more profound than any other dogma of the Christian faith. Failure to recognize its deepest meaning makes zeal for other aspects of the faith appear as vain, misconceived, or blind. The clamor for valid ministries and infallible scriptures undergoes a salutary transformation once the mystery of the cross is fully appreciated. Of course, without the meanings subsumed under the doctrines of the incarnation and the resurrection, the cross would not be the cross of Christ. The holy cross belongs in the total context of the evangelical and catholic faith. But within that context it forms the central point of reference.

Secondly, for Söderblom the cross of the Savior is the central symbol and mystery of Christianity around which all Christians could rally. The cross has a truly ecumenical appeal. Whether we find ourselves in a Roman Catholic, an Eastern Orthodox, or a Protestant church, in every case the cross crowns the highest point of the church structure. At the same time the holy cross symbolizes the deepest penetration into the mystery of the workings of the judgment and grace of God. Under the sign of the cross Christians in every section of Christendom celebrate the Eucharist in the mass, the divine liturgy, or the service of Holy Communion.

Thirdly, the mystery of the cross is for Archbishop Söderblom the mystery of vicarious suffering. It is the unique, Christian answer to the problem of evil and suffering in the world. Söderblom's studies of all the major living religions of the world led him to the inescapable conclusion that Christianity is the highest and special revelation of God, because it is the only religion in the world which has been able to give a positive answer and solution to the problem of suffering and evil. The cross, the cruel instrument of torture, suffering, shame, and death, has been transformed by Christianity into the noblest and highest hope of mankind. It discloses the divinely chosen way of redemption through vicarious suffering. In the final analysis, this kind of suffering is the only one that will reconcile man to God, and man to man. The holy cross reveals that, besides the solidarity of the human race in suffering, there is also the divine-human solidarity of atonement and blessing.

11. The World of Religion

Söderblom tended to see everything in its widest context. If each section of Christendom can be properly understood only as part of the one ecumenical church of Christ, then ecumenical Christianity as a whole must be seen in the context of all the other great religions of the world. Whatever else Christianity may be, it is undeniably one of the world's great religions. In a world that is ever drawing closer together, Christianity cannot afford to live in isolation. It must be ready for the encounter with the religions of the world. This is especially necessary in view of the fact that the Gospel must be preached to every creature under heaven. The majority of these creatures today are non-Christians. The crisis of Christianity on its traditional mission fields further highlights the relevance of Söderblom's appeal to reassess the traditional Christian attitudes toward non-Christian religions.

Archbishop Söderblom contended that a new look at the world's religions would greatly benefit the ecumenical spirit of Christianity. It would see itself in a wider context and thus get to know itself better. At the same time it would spearhead the effort to understand what is the place and function of religion in a secular world that has come of age. Not only Christianity, but the entire phenomenon of religion itself is called into question by the secular mind. Ecumenical theology and Christianity must therefore first try to know what religion is, and then what Christianity is within this general religious context. The alternative to Söderblom's proposal would be a secularization of the Gospel and the establishment of a religionless Christianity based on the premise that God is dead. Nathan Söderblom was convinced that the God-is-dead alternative is radically subversive to the ecumenical effort to promote Christian unity. At the same time he acknowledged freely that there have been times when God spoke to men through even those who denied his existence. In order to understand more clearly the thrust and relevance of Söderblom's contention that the encounter with the world's religions, in a spirit of understanding and good will, will not undermine the position of Christianity among the religions of the world, but rather bring out more clearly the unique and essentially ecumenical character of the Gospel, it is helpful to see the Söderblomian vision of ecumenicity in contrast to the concept of Christian unity based on a religionless Christianity. The prophet of a Christianity that is not a religion was the German Lutheran theologian Dietrich Bonhoeffer, who was martyred by Hitler's henchmen in one of the concentration camps of World War II. His ideas have been popularized by the Anglican bishop and theologian John A. T. Robinson. In his best-selling book *Honest to God*, Bishop Robinson calls for a recasting of the mold of Christianity into a worldly holiness and a new morality. In this country, similar ideas have been proposed by the Episcopal theologian Paul M. Van Buren, who has sought to state "the secular meaning of the gospel," and by men like Thomas J. J. Altizer and William Hamilton, whose main theme is that of the death of God.

The construction of an ecumenical theology on the basis of this new alternative to traditional Christianity is conceivable. Its universal appeal would presumably be its resolute denial of the relevance of religion for Christianity, and thus the elimination of the differences separating the various denominations by removing their religious basis.

A second reason for supposing that a secular restatement of the Gospel could expect a wide, interdenominational following is the universal presence and rapid expansion of secularism in every Christian denomination. If Christian unity is impossible on a religious basis, it might be successfully promoted on a secular one.

Thirdly, a reconstruction of Christianity on the premise that God is dead would enable Christians across denominational lines to adopt wholeheartedly a naturalistic framework. This framework would clarify or eliminate many traditional notions which are based on prescientific, supernaturalistic theologies, and which have become irrelevant and nonsensical in the technological and metropolitan world of man in the atomic and space age.

Archbishop Söderblom's ecumenical vision of Christian unity included the religious conception of Christianity. For him God was not dead; he was the living God. Söderblom believed that the existence of the living God could be proved by an objective and truthful effort to really understand the history of the religions of the world. Without the continued guidance and grace of God's Holy Spirit he could see no hope for the movement toward Christian unity. A united Christendom, the archbishop believed, would be needed to minister to a secular world torn by war and strife, by anxiety and hopelessness. The secular world cannot save itself. God alone can and must save it. And this God, who in various ways has manifested himself in every one of the religions of the world, is the God and Father of Christ, the Lord of the church. The prayer of the Lord, that his followers might be one as the Father and the Son are one, indicated to Söderblom that the source and prototype of ecumenical unity is the blessed Trinity. Hence the unity of the church cannot be built on the foundation of secular man in the secular city without reference to, or apart from, the God of the Christian religion. God is living and active in the process of ecumenicity. Far from being dead, God is the principle of the ecumenical concretion of Christian unity.

12. Dialogue with Rome

Throughout his ecumenical writings, Archbishop Söderblom was in dialogue with the Roman Catholic Church, "our great Roman sister church,"[13] as he liked to call it. One of his earlier writings had been devoted to a critical and constructive examination of the way in which the religious problem was understood in Roman Catholicism and in Protestantism. In this book of five hundred pages he examined the scope and impact of Roman Catholic modernism at the beginning of the twentieth century. He continued to engage in dialogue with Roman Catholicism until the end of his life. One of his last writings was devoted to an ecumenical dialogue with Max Pribilla, a Jesuit in Munich, Germany, who had written a history of the ecumenical conferences of Stockholm, in 1925, and of Lausanne, in 1927, from the Roman Catholic point of view. Toward the end of his comments about Pribilla's book, Söderblom expressed the hope that undignified polemics in the dialogue between Roman Catholics and Protestants would be replaced in our ecumenical era by exact and serious study, love of truth and mutual respect and understanding. With respect to the future Protestant attitude toward Rome, the archbishop desired the overcoming of confessional narrow-mindedness and the freedom to recognize and appreciate openly and frankly customs and saints in the Roman Catholic Church that are truly worthy of praise.

Söderblom was firmly convinced that the future of ecumenicity depended on the triumph of the spirit of good will and understanding between Roman Catholics on the one hand, and Orthodox and Protestants on the other. When Söderblom wrote this, in the early 1930's, this spirit was still very rare. Only today his ecumenical vision and hope is slowly being realized in the ecumenical encounter among various denominations on every continent on earth.

When the learned Jesuit Max Pribilla heard of the archbishop's death, he exclaimed: "May God resurrect the catholic Söderblom!" He had learned to love and respect in him a genuine evangelical catholic. For contemporary Christians today it would be a mistaken notion of evangelical catholicity if they were to seek to imitate slavishly the ecumenical example of Archbishop Söderblom. "The letter killeth, but the spirit giveth life." The abiding testament and heritage of Nathan Söderblom is and remains the ecumenical spirit of his evangelical and catholic vision of Christian unity.

NOTES

1. Second Vatican Council, *Decree on Ecumenism* (Glen Rock, N.J.: Paulist Press, 1965), p. 46.
2. Söderblom, *Christian Fellowship*, p. 123.
3. *Ibid.*, pp. 154-155.
4. *Ibid.*, p. 155.
5. Second Vatican Council, *Decree on Ecumenism*, p. 64.
6. *Ibid.*
7. Söderblom, *Christian Fellowship*, p. 123.
8. *Ibid.*
9. *Ibid.*, p. 145.
10. *Ibid.*, pp. 12-13.
11. Söderblom, "Why I Am a Lutheran," *Twelve Modern Apostles and Their Creeds*, pp. 78-79.
12. Nathan Söderblom, *Martin Luthers lilla katekes* (Stockholm: Svenska kyrkans diokonistyrelses bokförlag 1929), p. 213.
13. Nathan Söderblom, *Pater Max Pribilla und die ökumenische Erweckung* (Uppsala: Almquist & Wiksells boktryckeri, 1931), p. 99.

CHAPTER VII

CRITICISM AND CONCLUSION

The preceding pages have been devoted chiefly to a positive exposition of the life, thought, and lasting significance of Archbishop Nathan Söderblom. Few will doubt that he was a truly great ecumenical theologian and church leader. Many will grant that he was one of the most creative, knowledgeable, and illustrious historians of religion in the twentieth century. His writings will continue to inspire and guide theologians and sensitive laymen in the years ahead. However, in order to permit the reader to distinguish the lasting value of Söderblom's theological contribution from those phases of his life and thought that have only ephemeral and limited importance, it is necessary to present a comprehensive and objective survey of criticisms of his theology which have been made by some of the outstanding theologians of our century.

In all candor, however, the author feels that none of these criticisms is basic, profound, and incisive enough to discredit or invalidate Söderblom's tremendous contribution to the life and thought of the church in the twentieth century. Despite his critics, he still stands and is celebrated as one of the greatest religious leaders of modern times. For the sake of a complete understanding of Söderblom's impact on our century it is necessary to state exhaustively the critical reflections which his genius has aroused. But it is my conviction that Söderblom has outlived his critics and will continue to serve as a welcome harbor light to the churches battling the waves of change in the stormy waters of the spiritual revolution of our age.

In this last chapter is presented a complete summary of all the major criticisms of Söderblom that have been made over the years. Basically, there are twelve areas of critical reaction to Söderblomian theology and scholarship in the history of religions. Within this thematic arrangement appear the names of Söderblom's critics—among them such great theologians, philosophers, and historians as Gustaf Aulén, Paul Althaus, Emil Brunner, Adolf Harnack, and Ernst Troeltsch. Each of the twelve criticisms hurls a theological deathblow against Söderblom, but, like a man with thirteen lives, he survives them all. This shows what a theological giant he was, that he was able to be tested in the crucible of relentless criticism and then to arise more glorious than before.

The attentive reader will, no doubt, have gathered by now that I am a great admirer of Archbishop Söderblom, that I consider him one of the most creative theological minds and ecumenical leaders of our century, and that I basically disagree with his critics. At the same time I am humbly and apologetically aware that these disagreements with Söderblom's critics reflect my own concrete decisions on controversial theological, philosophical, and historical issues. As throughout the preceding chapters, so also in this last one I have been forced to employ certain theological and philosophical assumptions which I lack space to argue in detail: e.g., that reality is at bottom process, not static substance undergoing accidental change; that the basic theological problem of our time is that of the Gospel and modern man; that the ecumenical movement for Christian unity is a much needed reform movement within the churches.

Before moving to the twelve areas of criticism, a final word of explanation regarding their structure is necessary. Eight of them are clearly identified by the names of the critics whose views are presented there. Four of the themes of criticism are not explicitly attached to authors, originators, or chief exponents. In the latter cases I have momentarily assumed the role of a certain type of critic for the sake of completeness or in order to anticipate possible future criticisms. Thus in section 8 ("Liberalism") I have summarized the main objections of some minor conservative critics (like, for instance, Adolf Hult of Augustana Seminary, Rock Island, Illinois). Section 9 ("Monism") sums up the criticisms of a number of insignificant, conservative Scandinavian critics who were enamored with the motif of dualism. In section 11 ("Primacy of the Will") I have assumed, for the sake of argument, the viewpoint of Eastern

Orthodox Christianity, in order to anticipate possible criticisms from that perspective. Lastly, section 12 ("Pietism") is intended to reflect the possible criticisms of a hypothetical, skeptical, liberal, Protestant church historian. All of this, let me repeat again, has been done in order to present as objective and many-sided a picture of the life and work of Söderblom as possible. I myself consider the twelve criticisms to be either invalid, irrelevant, or too weakly argued.

1. Disorderliness

A major source of misunderstanding, difficulty, and contradictions is the disorderliness of Söderblom's method of presenting any given subject. In some of his major writings the chaotic welter of thoughts obscures the main point of the discussion and leaves the reader and student of Söderblom in a state of confusion and intellectual frustration. A number of admirers of Söderblom have voiced the same criticism. Bishop Eivind Berggrav in his tribute to Söderblom's genius and character noted the archbishop's carelessness in the ordering of his thoughts. He was wont to collect ideas, and when he had enough for a book, he published the material without making careful revisions of his writings prior to publication. His method of working with ideas was such that it left almost every idea incomplete and disorderly.

A similar complaint of disorderliness is made by Folke Holmström, who devoted a massive work of over four hundred pages to a study of Söderblom's concept of revealed religion and mysticism (*Uppenbarelsereligion och mystik*; Stockholm, 1937). Holmström demonstrated that the archbishop tended to blur the very distinctions which he had taken great pains to clarify.

In his memorial article on Nathan Söderblom as a theologian, Gustaf Aulén pointed out correctly that Söderblom's lack of orderly and systematic thinking prevented him from noticing Ritschlian materials in his theological structure which do not really fit there. There is a lack of harmony, especially in the later writings of the archbishop, due to statements which clearly bear traces of Ritschlian influence, and which cannot be harmonized with the rest of Söderblom's theological position.

2. History of Religions

Serious questions can be raised with regard to the appropriateness of much of the material drawn from the history of religions in relation to Söderblom's theology. Do they really add anything to his theology except confusion and ultimately irrelevant sidetracks? Both from the point of view of the history of religions and from the standpoint of Christian theology Söderblom's method is highly questionable. There are times when he uses the history of religions in a way which is historically untenable and theologically indefensible. He tries to combine the history of religions and Christian theology in an impossible manner. A most basic criticism of Söderblom's entire approach and method was raised by the famous church historian Adolf von Harnack. Harnack contended that the attempt to include the study of the history of religions in the field of Christian theology is destructive of the continued vitality and relevance of theology, because theology would get lost in the study of the religions of the world and their historical development. Söderblom in his examination of the relationship between the religious historian and the theologian (*Den allmänna religionshistorien och den kyrkliga teologien*) advanced the thesis that theology must study the history of religions in its entire scope in order to be able to understand the nature of religion and the uniqueness of Christianity in the context of the world's religions.

Harnack's criticism of the Söderblomian perspective was based on the conviction that Christian theology must not get involved in the study of the history of religions because theology has a much more important task. Its proper and only real function is the better clarification of the genuine essence of Christianity. The historical and critical study of the non-Christian religions of the world is completely unnecessary to the successful fulfillment of this function of theology. To know the Christian religion is to know all religions, because Christianity comprises within itself virtually all important and significant characteristics and dynamisms of religion.

The Swiss theologian Emil Brunner made a related criticism of Söderblom's idea that the history of religions is necessary for the wellbeing of theology. In his book on *Natural Religion and the His-*

tory of Religion (Naturlig religion och religionshistoria) Söderblom had proposed that from now on theology should substitute the objective and critical study of the history of religions for the old, traditional notion of natural religion and natural theology. Traditional Christian reflection has occupied itself with the notion of natural theology in order to give recognition to that knowledge of God which can be obtained by observing the visible processes of nature. It claims that the inner response of man to the outward condition and circumstance of life and his capability to observe the visible processes of nature are a means by which he can discover the meaning of his existence and the obligations under which he lives. Furthermore, it is believed by the champions of natural religion and natural theology that the more man obeys and follows the tendency of nature toward a moral government, the greater is the happiness which he can realize. The way to come to happiness is to come ever closer to a complete harmony with the moral law.

According to natural theology, as man obeys the natural law he internalizes the moral law until it becomes categorical. Once this state of progress is achieved, man is essentially a law unto himself, and he is obliged to this law because it is the law of nature. The connection between the traditional interpretation of natural theology and the idea of natural religion consists in the claim that genuine natural religion acknowledges no other authority than natural theology. The problem for the Christian theologian traditionally has been that of the relation between reason and natural religion on the one hand, and faith and revelation on the other.

Söderblom approached this problem as a historian. He asked himself whether as a historian he could find anywhere in the world a living religion that could be called "natural," a religion which could be studied and observed in its theory and its practice. But not even among the most primitive tribes and men did he find anything that corresponded even approximately to the traditional notion of natural religion. He therefore came to the conclusion that natural religion did not in fact exist, but was a product of speculative thought. In order to ground the concept of revelation in the concretely and historically existing evidences of divine revelation, Söderblom demanded that Christian theology empirically test its concepts against the correlative religious realities in other actually existing religions of mankind. The history of non-Christian religions must therefore replace the abstract, speculative, and nonhistorical notion of natural religion. The traditional interpretations of natural religion and natural theology were in Söderblom's view a work of fiction. Natural theology and natural religion did not really exist, except as an unreal abstraction from the historical, positive reality of a plurality of religions.

Brunner, in his book on *The Philosophy of Religion,* maintained that the preoccupation with the history of religions on the part of theologians like Söderblom is the reflection of an ephemeral fad. The history of religions was a burning issue in the last third of the nineteenth and the first third of the twentieth centuries, but, like every fashion, it had its day and now has passed into relative obscurity. The problem of the relationship between reason and revelation, which was the central problem of the old notion of natural theology, will remain a crucial question long after it has ceased to dominate theological interest. Söderblom's program is therefore leading theology astray into unnecessary irrelevancies. Perhaps under the influence of existentialism, Brunner based his criticism of Söderblom on the observation that the problem of the history of religions and Christian revelation raised a purely theoretical issue which did not really and vitally affect human existence. With the possible exception of the light it could throw on the conflict between mysticism and Christian faith, Söderblom's thesis of the importance of the history of religions for theology lacked existential relevance.[1]

Brunner believed that the discovery of the spiritual and religious treasures of the Eastern religions during the past century had for the first time made accessible to Christian thinkers religious materials which were vastly superior to the religious systems of classical antiquity. Hence the excitement of Söderblom and other historians of religion around the turn of the twentieth century. But now that theologians have gotten used to the Eastern and primitive religions of the world, and have learned that there are non-Christian religions of great power, the time has come for them to return to their own proper task, that of Christian theology. Söderblom had his day, but now he is definitely *passé,* whereas the problem of natural theology, of reason and revelation, today is a more burning question than ever before in the history of the church and of Christian thought.

3. The Uniqueness of Christianity

Söderblom expended a great deal of effort to demonstrate the absolutely unique character of Christianity by means of a historical investigation of the religions of the world. He believed that he had found a historical proof of the existence of God, in addition to the traditional cosmological and teleological and ontological arguments for the existence of God. By means of the history of religions he believed that he could prove that there is a living God and that Christianity is absolutely unique among the religions of man. This view of Söderblom is open to the criticism that the objective and historically critical study of the history of religions cannot and must not function as a substitute for faith. The God of Christian faith is simply not subject to historical proof.

The well-known theologian Ernst Troeltsch criticized the attempt of Söderblom and other theologians who endeavored to demonstrate the absolute and unique character of the Christian religion. In his famous work on the absolute character of Christianity and the history of religions *(Die Absolutheit des Christentums und die Religionsgeschichte)* Troeltsch contended that a historical approach to religion could not demonstrate the absolute and unique nature of the Christian religion for two reasons. First, the tools of historical and critical research make it impossible to prove the absolute character of any religion. In the history of religions everything is relative and related, nothing is absolute or unrelated. Secondly, the general ideas necessary to establish the absolute or absolutely unique character of any religion are irreconcilably opposed to the concretely individual and historically relative structures and realities of religion. Söderblom therefore could not demonstrate the uniqueness or absolute nature of Christianity from the history of religions without either distorting historical facts or doing violence to the Christian faith. Throughout the writings of Söderblom there are occasional indications that he was aware of this criticism, probably the most devastating criticism of all. But he never defended himself against it; indeed, he was rather defenseless against any kind of unfriendly criticism. His great strength was not defense, but offense in the sense of constructive outreach.

4. Contradictions

Even if we proceed from the Söderblomian assumption that the uniqueness of Christianity can be demonstrated by means of the study of the history of religions, there still remains room for criticism of the way in which Söderblom went about the task of showing that Christianity is unique and that it is the fulfillment of all religion and revelation. At certain points his contention that there is a genuine, general revelation in all the religions of the world is simply irreconcilable with the view that Christianity is the perfect religion of revelation. The Swedish theologian Erland Ehnmark, in his examination of the religious problem in Söderblom's thought *(Religionsproblemet hos Nathan Söderblom)*, argued, for instance, that out of Söderblom's attempts to adjust the tensions between his emphasis on the uniqueness of Christian revelation and on the general revelation of God in all religions, in history, and in genius, arise some of the most baffling and characteristic problems in his concept of revelation.

For example, Söderblom's position raises the question as to what exactly it is that the non-Christian religions reveal. He insisted that they reveal the living God whose existence could be proved through the history of religions. He further emphasized that in biblical history the revelation of God is more important and richer than revelation in any other religious history. But on this basis the uniqueness of Christianity cannot be defended. If the difference between Christianity and non-Christian religions is only a matter of more or less, something altogether relative, it is impossible to show that Christianity is unique whereas all other religions are not.

The same criticism must be made of Söderblom's distinction between the mysticism of personality and the mysticism of infinity. According to Söderblom, the nonbiblical religions, except Mazdaism and Islam, are dominated by the mysticism of infinity which seeks the revelation of God not in history, but outside of history and time.

Mysticism receives the revelation of God through communion with deity. The infinity mystic sees the divine as an impersonal power, the nameless, holy One, the infinite Unity, the changeless, all-embracing Beginning and End of all things. History, change, time, process are illusory; thus the mysticism of infinity beclouds the revelation of God. Nevertheless, the vision of God as the changeless One who transcends history and time belongs also to the Christian conception of God. The decisive thing for the biblical concept of God, however, is that he reveals himself in history, in change, and in time. According to Söderblom's idea of religion and revelation, the mysticism of personality seeks communion with deity by involvement in history and accords a crucial role to personality. Through this personal, historical communion with God, the prophets, Jesus, the apostles and saints received and discerned revelation in history.

In Söderblom's opinion the mysticism of personality is most ideally suited to apprehend the full meaning of the Gospel, because it looks for revelation in historical events and in human personality. Jesus Christ is the fulfillment of revelation because in him the revelation of God in history is incarnate. The uniqueness of Christianity is that the highest revelation of the divine comes in the form of a historical revealer, the incarnate Word, and the mystery of the cross. It may be granted that Söderblom's distinction between types of mysticism has some merit, but these types do not establish the uniqueness of Christianity. The historical reality of Christian religion comprises both the mysticism of infinity and the mysticism of personality. The difference between Christianity and other religions in this respect is a relative matter and not something that could establish the uniqueness of Christianity among the world's religions.

In an article on holiness written for the *Encyclopedia of Religion and Ethics,* Söderblom advanced the thesis that holiness rather than the concept of God is the touchstone of religion. Primitive religions sometimes do not have a god-concept, but they are aware of the reality of the holy as the core and basis of the essence of religion. Higher religions like Buddhism also may not involve a belief in God or gods. Yet they are religions. Consequently the idea of the holy, rather than the concept of deity, is the criterion of religion. This view of the essence of religion as constituted by the idea of holiness is poorly suited to support Söderblom's notion of the uniqueness of Christianity. There may be differing forms in which the consciousness of the holy expresses itself in the various religions, but on that basis no claim to genuine uniqueness can be sustained by any one of the religions of the world.

Students of Söderblom have also noted that in his efforts to show the uniqueness of Christianity among the world's religions Söderblom tended to pick certain elements of Christian faith and to omit others. Charles J. Adams,[2] among others, has pointed out that the Christian religion is too complex and many-sided to be forced into the typological mold of "revealed religion" *(uppenbarelsereligion)* which Söderblom had prepared for it. Much of historical and contemporary Christianity reminds the objective observer more of nature and culture religions than of revealed religion. Christianity must thus be seen as a highly complex religion containing within itself almost every type and variation of religious experience. But the example of Islam indicates that Christianity is by no means unique in this regard. The type of "religion of revelation" as distinct from "culture religion" or "nature religion" is on Söderblom's own grounds not the unique type of Christian religion, and hence not very helpful in bringing out the unique essence of Christianity.

5. Idealism

In his statements about the nature of revelation and the essence of Christianity, Söderblom was not always sufficiently careful. Non-Christian, humanistic notions and echoes of idealism are sometimes indiscriminately mixed with genuinely Christian elements. His statements about genius as a portal of revelation strike the reader often as little more than an idealization of human nature. The cult of personality, the worship of genius, and the veneration of heroes are carelessly thrown together with evangelical and kerygmatic Christian ideas in a strange mixture of idealism and evangelical revival piety. Gustaf Wingren, in his essay on *Swedish Theology Since 1900,* was critical of Söderblom's failure to be sufficiently sensitive to the opposition of Christianity on the one hand to humanism and on the other hand to the old Protestant orthodoxy. Others have made similar observations, remarking critically that the work of Söderblom lacks the depths of awareness of this double opposition, and hence is at certain points somewhat out of focus. This fuzziness is especially noticeable when Söderblom attempts to show the basic differences between biblical faith in God and other religious, philosophical, mystical, and secular concepts of the divine.

In the context of a discussion of Söderblom's idea of continued revelation, Gustaf Aulén, in his memorial essay on Nathan Söderblom as a theologian, voiced the criticism that some of Söderblom's statements about evolution, progress, and continuity in revelation were not truly Christian. Söderblom's concept of revelation through genius, for instance, stands side by side with the regenerating and sanctifying power of the grace of God. In some aspects the Söderblomian understanding of continued revelation through genius, history, and the moral urge to ideals of conduct is made synonymous with the idealization of human nature. This way of interpreting revelation is, however, rooted in idealism rather than in biblical and genuinely Christian thought. A similar criticism must be made of his statements about the progress and process of continued revelation in the last chapter of his book on *The Religious Problem in Catholicism and Protestantism.* Söderblom there used ideas and categories quite obviously taken from Bergsonian process thought, mixed them up with biblical and Christian concepts of faith, and presented a theologically very questionable statement of some of the essentials of Christian faith. There is no doubt that the idea of progressive process of revelation had been a much neglected element of genuine Christianity, and that Söderblom sought to emphasize the ever living and active God of biblical revelation. The way in which he did this, however, was, as Aulén already noted, theologically out of focus.

6. Doctrine

In many of Söderblom's ecumenical writings there is a noticeable tendency to stress practical Christianity at the expense of concern for Christian truth and doctrines. Related to the cult of genius as one of the portals of divine revelation is the emphasis on personality and history rather than Scripture and doctrine as loci of divine revelation, in the past as well as in the contemporary ecumenical process. The Lutheran theologian Paul Althaus criticized Söderblom because the critical, theological categories of truth and error were not sufficiently developed by Söderblom's ecumenical mind. From his historical perspective Söderblom tended to see the divisions of Christendom as members of the body of Christ. But these members did not recognize that they really belonged together as members of the one body of Christ. Söderblom therefore tended to stress, on the one hand, the value of preserving the historically distinct and diverse forms of Christianity (Anglicanism, Lutheranism, Calvinism, Roman Catholicism, Eastern Orthodoxy, etc.), and, on the other hand, the unification of these members in freedom. Althaus criticized this view as both unrealistic and unfaithful to the Lutheran point of view, which considers the question of pure doctrine and right teaching, as well as the right administration of the sacraments, to be of crucial importance for all Christian denominations, not just for the Lutheran ones. How unacceptable the Söderblomian ecumenism was to the Roman Catholic Church could be seen by the papal encyclical *Mortalium animos*, which denounced Söderblom's ecumenical theory and practice as the unholy work of dangerous *panchristiani*. The question of truth and error could not be so simply reduced to a mere matter of different historical development and perspective.

7. Psychology

In his books dealing with the history of religions, in his strictly theological and devotional works, as well as in his Luther studies, Söderblom had a predilection for the psychology of religious experience. The psychologizing trend at several points threatened to undermine the theological foundation on which Söderblom sought to construct his thought. This is quite obvious in his typology of religion and religious experience. For this reason criticisms must be made of his notions of "revealed religion" and "mysticism of personality." Conrad Bergendoff, in his Harvard Lecture on *The Sphere of Revelation*, complained about the theological ambiguity of the notion of "revealed religion."[3] The contemporary meaning of the term "religion" is used to cover a great deal of nonsense, superstition, emotional phantasy, and delusion. Psychologically speaking, the Christian believer may be very sincere in his belief that all this is "revealed religion," but for a serious-minded theologian it is not proper to use the word revelation to coat over the cruelty, inhumanity, and nonsense that religion has produced. From the point of view of the religious psychologist the Christian claim that his religion has been revealed as the true religion may be helpful in the psychological interpretation of religious experience, but for theology this could only mean that the indispensable rational and critical criteria have been removed. And once these criteria are gone or relegated to a secondary place there is no way to insure a valid distinction between truth and delusion. The term "revealed religion" implies that there is revelation of a religion. From a theological point of view, however, there is revelation of the living God, and Christian religion is the human response to this revelation (a response that often sullies and distorts divine revelation), but there is no revelation of a religion.

Questions can also be raised as to the legitimacy of the word "mysticism of personality." From a psychological point of view the religious type of infinity mysticism may be of helpful, descriptive value; theologically speaking, however, this notion is untenable unless it is simply another word for faith in the sense in which Martin Luther used it. In his memorial essay on Söderblom's theology Gustaf Aulén recognized that the Söderblomian mysticism of personality basically refers to nothing more than the inward aspect of faith as living fellowship with God. To call this mysticism is misleading theologically, and superfluous semantically.

8. Liberalism

Throughout Söderblom's writings runs a noticeable split between the Gospel, on the one hand, and the doctrines of the church on the other. There are places where he goes out of his way to stress that a certain doctrine is directly opposed to the kerygma. Partly this antidogmatic stance must be understood as the heritage of revivalism and pietism in its opposition to the confessional Protestant orthodoxy of the times. Partly Söderblom is a child of the antidogmatic liberalism of the nineteenth and early twentieth centuries. Just as the Ritschlian liberal Adolf von Harnack interpreted the emergence of church dogma as the fall of the church from kerygmatic innocence, so Söderblom, in his own way, shared the prejudice that the doctrines of the church are for the most part more or less clearly opposed to the evangelical spirit of the early church. But at the same time, where it suited his purpose, he would pick out certain doctrines and emphases of confessional orthodoxy, and triumphantly announce his rediscovery of basic truths found already in the doctrinal statements of Lutheran orthodoxy. Thus, for instance, the old orthodox doctrine of the *communicatio idiomatum,* which said that even in the perfect revelation of God in Christ the human and the divine are commingled, was recovered by Söderblom because it fitted in with his humanistic concern and emphasis. And when he discovered that the "angelic doctor" of Lutheran orthodoxy, Johann Gerhard, had called his statement of Lutheran doctrines a "catholic confession" *(Confessio catholica),* Söderblom proclaimed immediately that his catholic sympathies had the full support of the greatest of the old Lutheran orthodox dogmaticians. From both a historical and a theological standpoint this quite arbitrary interpretation and appropriation of Christian doctrine is enough to make the critical reader of Söderblom wary at certain points.

9. Monism

Söderblom made a great deal of the "dualism" of prophetic and biblical religion. Whereas culture and nature religions tend to be monistic, prophetic religions (Mazdaism, Judaism, Christianity, Islam) are dualistic. Prophetic religion lives in the world of struggle between ultimate and opposing forces: the leader of the hosts of light, Ahura Mazda, against the spirit of darkness, Angra Mainya or Ahriman, in Mazdaism; Elijah, the prophet of God against the prophets of Baal; Christ against the demonic forces of the devil; the servants of Allah against the unbelievers. When Söderblom outlines his own theological position, however, his stance is basically monistic rather than dualistic. There exists an inherent contradiction between the monism of the cross, which for him is the central dogma of Christian faith, and his findings in the history of religions, which point to an essentially dualistic emphasis within Christianity. Söderblom's onesided stress on the doctrine of the atonement—or "the mystery of vicarious suffering" as he called it—does not do justice to the double dialectic, on the one hand, of the incarnation and the cross, and on the other hand, of the cross and the resurrection. His monism of the cross reflects partly the erosion in Lutheranism of any meaningful concept of the incarnation, and partly the disappearance of the significance of the resurrection since the enlightenment, especially in the liberalism of the late nineteenth century.

10. Rationalism

Closely related to the Söderblomian monism of Christ's suffering on the cross is his attack upon the traditional notion that God cannot suffer. This was his way of attacking the old idea of the transcendence of God. It indicated the beginning erosion of any meaningful concept of divine transcendence, and the concomitant emphasis on the humanity of God in Christ. The more conservative and orthodox Lutheran churchmen and theologians were naturally quite perturbed about this brand of "liberalism" and "rationalism" as they called it. One of the leading critics of Söderblom was the Archbishop of Finland, Gustaf Johansson. He felt that Söderblom, in whose concept of revelation the notion of vicarious suffering is given greater emphasis as the central mystery of Christianity than the virgin birth, or the descent into hell, or the bodily resurrection of Christ, or the divinity of the person of the Holy Spirit, had not sufficiently dissociated himself from rationalist tendencies. In Johansson's opinion this failure of Söderblom to take seriously the supernatural and transcendent elements of Christian faith was bound up with Söderblom's ecumenical desire to communicate with fellow Christians across denominational walls. The common experience of suffering, which all had experienced during the First World War, was to rally all Christians around the sign of the cross. The uniting force of common suffering and the universal challenge of human need were in Söderblom's view more likely to help the cause of Christian unity than doctrinal agreement on the doctrine of the virgin birth or the bodily resurrection of Christ from the dead.

Johansson criticized Söderblom's unwillingness to make the Apostles' Creed the basis and requisite of ecumenism and Christian cooperation. For Söderblom the creed had lost meaning in its literal and transcendental sense. It failed to confirm or to elucidate human experience in the twentieth century, except for the statements about suffering. Existential relevance was the Söderblomian criterion for theological truth. Johansson denounced this as the nefarious attempt of rationalism to crush the creed of the church. His evaluation of what transpired at the ecumenical Stockholm Conference, in 1925, under the leadership of Söderblom, criticized the attenuation or outright disregard of the proper, transcendental meaning of the revelation of God in Jesus Christ, with the resulting weakening of the standing of Christ in the world. The kerygma of the church is reduced by rationalism to the point where it tells the world nothing that the world cannot tell itself. Thus the salt of the earth has lost its taste, and the percentage of the world's population which still finds the message of the church meaningful decreases day by day. Rationalism may mean the great liberation for the theological student or professor struggling to maintain his intellectual honesty (Söderblom had this experience when reading Ritschlian theology), but for the church it is the kiss of death. This was the basic criticism of Archbishop Johansson of Finland.

11. Primacy of the Will

In his studies of Christianity and other religions of the world, Söderblom concluded that the notion of God as will was the characteristic and unique emphasis of prophetic and biblical religions. The stress that God is will exercising itself in history and in the inner life of personality is to be explained partly as a reflection of the existential makeup of Söderblom. His contemporaries knew him as a man of unbending will, and it was only natural that he should find this notion quite meaningful. Partly the elevation of will as the central agency of human and divine action and understanding is the reflection of a Western theological preoccupation and prejudice. St. Augustine made the category of will central for the Western theological tradition. But in the East the will never held a position of similar importance, and in the West there are other traditions which do not place the will in the center of theological focus. The somewhat provincial emphasis on God as will is thus in marked contradiction to Söderblom's otherwise universal and ecumenical stance.

12. Pietism

Söderblom liked to think of himself as a catholic church leader and theologian. His particular brand of catholicity was evangelical; however, he was not simply an evangelical but rather an evangelical catholic. There is a certain kind of inconsistency and even incoherence in the catholic tendency wedded to a pietistic concern with the cross and suffering of Jesus. At a number of points the Söderblomian emphasis on the cross is not catholic but reflects the sentimental, almost sick, blood-of-Jesus piety of nineteenth-century evangelical revivalism.

When it came to the cross, which Söderblom declared to be the one and only center of his theology, the ecumenical archbishop tended to become quite intolerant and exclusive. Against those who emphasized the great doctrines and tradition of the church catholic, and against those who called for a return to biblical categories as the one and only salvation of theology and the church, he declared that "there is *one* dogma that is weightier than all the rest. He who stands in the presence of this dogma and does not know what it means may be as zealous as possible for the literal inspiration of the Bible, for dogmas and tradition—it is all of little use, if in any degree he obscures the real essence of Christianity, which is the Mystery of the Cross, our highest, nay our only hope in life and in death."[4] The basic reason why the cross is the one dogma of Christianity is that it has existential significance for contemporary man. "No rationalism, ancient or modern, can ever take the place of the inexhaustible drama of Christianity, which embraces all history, of the race and of the individual, and gives it meaning. Its center and climax is at Calvary. But it continues in every generation, in the mysterious spiritual solidarity, which, alike for suffering and for redemption, unites mankind with invisible bonds. In our Christian fellowship there is continually reproduced something of the mystery of the Cross, wherever one suffers for another's sin, with a love that manifests something of God's power. This drama must in its degree be continued in the story of every human soul. This, and this only, is Christianity."[5]

There is no question but that this exclusive emphasis on the cross reflects a narrow concern rooted in nineteenth-century Swedish pietism, revivalism, and evangelicalism. Clearly it cannot be seriously proposed as the one and only essence of Christianity. The Anglican emphasis on the incarnation, the Roman Catholic institutional emphasis on sacramental grace, the Eastern Orthodox vision of the apotheosis, the deification of man ("God became man in order that man might become God," said St. Athanasius of Alexandria, one of the great and formative theologians and church leaders of the East), and the Lutheran stress on justification are examples sufficient to indicate that the question of the "real essence of Christianity," as Söderblom called it, is more complex than he was willing to admit.

These criticisms are not meant to depreciate the work and significance of Archbishop Nathan Söderblom. They are rather meant to bring out more clearly his real contribution to the life and thought of contemporary Christianity. No theologian is perfect, and those who study his works to find guidance and inspiration in them must learn to distinguish truth from error and gold from fool's gold. Critical readings in Söderblom also help the contemporary reader to see him in his historical context, and thus facilitate understanding of his life and thought. The critical awareness of possible pitfalls and dangers in certain of Söderblom's emphases will help later theologians and thoughtful laymen to keep Christian truth in its proper context and perspective, and thus avoid seizing upon one aspect of a man's thought, taking it out of its context, and making the part appear as though it were the whole.

Finally, it is to be remembered that while the right and duty of critical judgment cannot and must not be suspended, the lasting contributions of Söderblom are those which will continue to attract men and capture their minds and wills. He will be remembered for the good he did rather than for the mistakes he made. His creative concern for ecumenicity, peace, renewal, and universal understanding of all the religions of the world will continue to be a guiding star for Christian faith and life in the years ahead.

NOTES

1. Emil Brunner, *The Philosophy of Religion*, trans. A. J. D. Farrer and Bertram Lee Woolf (New York: Charles Scribner's Sons, 1937), pp. 127-28.
2. Charles J. Adams, "Nathan Söderblom as an Historian of Religions" (Unpublished Ph.D. dissertation, Divinity School, University of Chicago, 1955), p. 238.
3. Conrad Bergendoff, "The Sphere of Revelation," *Harvard Divinity School Bulletin, Number 14, Official Register of Harvard University*, XLVI, No. 10 (April 25, 1949), 22.
4. Nathan Söderblom, *The Mystery of the Cross*, trans., A. G. Hebert (Milwaukee: Morehouse Publ. Co., 1933), p. 31.
5. *Ibid.*, pp. 30-31.

Bibliography in English

The complete list of Söderblom's writings includes over 700 items which have been published in several languages. In addition to this there is a wealth of literature about Söderblom in many languages. The following bibliography includes only those books and articles by and about Archbishop Söderblom published in the English language.

WRITINGS BY SÖDERBLOM

Nathan Söderblom. *The Nature of Revelation.* Edited and with an introduction by Edgar M. Carlson. Philadelphia: Fortress Press, 1966.

"Ages of the World (Zoroastrian)," *Encyclopedia of Religion and Ethics,* ed. J. Hastings (1908), I, 205-210.

"Ardashir I," *Encyclopedia of Religion and Ethics,* ed. J. Hastings (1908), I, 774.

"The Place of the Christian Trinity and the Buddhist Triratna amongst Holy Triads," *Transactions of the Third International Congress for the History of Religions* (Oxford, 1908), II, 391-410.

"Ascetism (Persian)," *Encyclopedia of Religion and Ethics,* ed. J. Hastings (1909), II, 105-106.

"Father, Son and Holy Spirit, Their Relationships in Modern Thought," *Jesus or Christ? Essays (The Hibbert Journal,* 1908/09 Supplement), VII, 147-164.

"Communion with Deity (Introductory, Parsi)," *Encyclopedia of Religion and Ethics,* ed. J. Hastings (1910), III, 736-740; 776.

"The Student Movement of Sweden," *The Student World* (1910), pp. 121-126.

"Creed (Parsi)," *Encyclopedia of Religion and Ethics,* ed. J. Hastings (1911), IV, 247-248.

"Death and Disposal of the Dead (Parsi)," *Encyclopedia of Religion and Ethics,* ed. J. Hastings (1911), IV, 502-505.

"Does God Continue to Reveal Himself to Mankind?" *Report of the Conference of the World's Student Christian Federation* (Constantinople and London, 1911), pp. 59-78.

"Holiness (General and Primitive)," *Encyclopedia of Religion and Ethics,* ed. J. Hastings (1913), VI, 731-741.

"Incarnation (Introductory; Parsi)," *Encyclopedia of Religion and Ethics,* ed. J. Hastings (1914), VII, 183-84.

"On the Character of the Swedish Church," *The Constructive Quarterly* (1915), III, 281-310.

"On the Soul of the Church of Sweden," *The Constructive Quarterly* (1915), III, 506-545.

"An International Church Conference," *The Challenge* (1917), VIII, 55-56.

"Greeting to the American Lutheran Church in View of the 400th Anniversary of the Reformation," *The Lutheran* (Nov. 8, 1917), p. 3

"Our Spiritual Peril as Neutrals," *The Constructive Quarterly* (1917), V, 91-96.

"Theopompus and the Avestan Ages of the World," *Dastur Hoshang Memorial Volume* (Bombay, 1918), pp. 228-230.

"Vermin and Holiness," *Dastur Hoshang Memorial Volume* (Bombay, 1918), pp. 226-227.

Easter (Chicago: Covenant Book Concern, 1930).

Memorandum Presented to the International Committee of the World Alliance for Promoting International Friendship through the Churches at The Hague, October 2nd, 1919 (Uppsala, 1920).

"Christian Missions and National Politics," *The International Review of Missions* (1919), VIII, 491-499.

"The Church and International Goodwill," *The Contemporary Review* (1919), CXVI, 309-315.

"The Unity of Christendom," *American Scandinavian Review* (1920), VIII, 585-592.

"The United Life and Work of Christendom," *The Christian World Pulpit* (London, 1921), IC, 210-212.

On the Reconstruction of European Civilization (Uppsala, 1923).

"The Church in Sweden," *The Swedish Yearbook* (Uppsala, 1922), pp. 53-58.

"The League of Nations Needs a Christian Soul," *The British Weekly* (Oct. 5, 1922).

Christian Fellowship (Chicago: Revell, 1923).

"Evangelic Catholicity," *The Lutheran Church Review* (1924), XLIII, 1-10.

"Martin Luther's Universal Significance," *The Lutheran* (1924), VI, 11-13, 24.

"The Cathedral of St. John the Divine," *The Augustana Quarterly* (1924), III, 111-123.

"The Three Great Surprises," *The Christian World Pulpit* (1924), CVI, 91-92.

"A Conversation in a Motor-Car," *The Forum* (1924), LXXII.

"Religion in a Ford," *The Forum* (1924), LXXII, 330-338.

"A Message from Sweden," *Mobilizing for Peace,* ed. F. Lynch (New York and Chicago, 1924), pp. 233-246.

"Life and Work," *The Review of the Churches* (New Series; 1925), II, 184-189.

"The Church in England and Sweden," *The Swedish-British Society Yearbook 1924* (Stockholm, 1925), pp. 7-11.

"Why Rome Makes Converts," *The Review of the Churches* (New Series; 1924), I, 463-470.

"The Inner Guest," *The Christian Work* (New York, 1924), CXVI, 524-526.

"The Problem of Alcohol," *The Stockholm Conference 1925,* ed. G. K. A. Bell (London, 1926), pp. 405-413.

"Mobilizing the Forces of the Church," *Goodwill* (July 15, 1925).

"Why I Am a Lutheran," *Twelve Modern Apostles and Their Creeds* (New York, 1926), pp. 72-88.

"Christ the Ruler," *The Christian World Pulpit* (1926), CX, 31-33.

"Echo of Stockholm," *The Review of the Churches* (New Series; 1926), III, 351-353.

"New and Old," *The Congregationalist* (1926), CXI, 8-9.

"The Child in Our Day," *An Outline of Christianity* (New York, 1926), V. 28-35.

Conflicting Loyalties Confronting Christian Youth Today (Geneva: Atar, 1927).

"A Letter on Helsingfors," *The Sphere* (1927), VII, 2-3.

"The Historic Christian Fellowship," *Report of the Jerusalem Meeting of the International Missionary Council, March 24th-April 8th, 1928*, III, 133-154.

The Church and Peace (Oxford, 1929).

"The Church of Sweden," *The Reunion of Christendom*, ed. J. Marchant (London: 1929), pp. 85-102.

"The Trinity Season," *The British Weekly* (1929), LXXXVI, 225-226.

"If We Are Not to Have Another War," *Federal Council Bulletin* (Jan., 1929).

The Mystery of the Cross (Milwaukee: Morehouse Publishing Co., 1933).

The Nature of Revelation (New York: Oxford University Press, 1933).

The Living God (London: Oxford University Press, 1933).

"Assurance in Religion," *The Commemoration Volume of the Science of Religion* (Tokyo: Imperial University, 1934), pp. 220-227.

ENGLISH WRITINGS ABOUT SÖDERBLOM

Aulén, Gustaf. "Nathan Söderblom as a Theologian," *Church Quarterly Review*, (October, 1932), CXV, 15-48.

Bergendoff, Conrad. "Nathan Söderblom, Archbishop and Evangelical Catholic," *Una Sancta* (1965), XXII, 2-17.

Curtis, C. J. *Facets of Ecumenicity*. Fresno, California: Academy Guild Press, 1966.

———— "Apostle of Christian Unity," *Lutheran Witness Reporter* (1966), II, 5.

———— "An Ecumenical Churchman," *The Lutheran Standard*, VI, 12.

———— "Archbishop Söderblom on Theology and the History of Religions," *The Anglican*, XXII, No. 4 (Winter, 1966), 6-13.

———— "Choose Your Trinity," *The Anglican*, XXII, No. 3 (Autumn, 1966), 2-11.

———— "Nathan Söderblom's Conception of Christ as the Fulfillment of Revelation," *The Lutheran Quarterly*, XVII, 252-259.

———— "Nathan Söderblom's Concept of Revelation as Individual and Social Wholeness," *American Church Quarterly*, VI, No. 1 (Spring, 1966), 33-44.

———— "Nathan Söderblom: Pope John of Protestant Ecumenism," *The American Ecclesiastical Review*, CLVI, No. 1 (January, 1967), 1-9.

——— "Nathan Söderblom's Concept of Revelation Through Saint and Genius," *Covenant Quarterly,* XXIV, No. 3, (August, 1966), 3-13.

——— "Peacemaker in the Name of God," *The National Lutheran* (1966), XXIV, 10-12.

——— "Söderblom: Ecumenical Churchman and Theologian," *The Christian Century* (1966) LXXXIII, 47-48.

——— " 'The Living God' Theology," *The Ecumenist,* V, No. 1 (November-December, 1966), 1-3.

——— "Theologian of Revelation," *The Living Church,* CLII, 2-5.

——— "The True and the Beautiful: Nathan Söderblom's Concept of Revelation Through Music and Art," *Una Sancta,* XXII, 38-43.

——— "Nathan Söderblom and America," *The Swedish Pioneer Historical Quarterly,* XVII, 101-104.

——— "Nathan Söderblom's Concept of Revelation Through Saint and Genius," *The Covenant Quarterly* (August, 1966).

——— *Nathan Söderblom: Theologian of Revelation.* Chicago: Covenant Press, 1966.

Ehnmark, Erland. "General Revelation According to Nathan Söderblom," *The Journal of Religion,* XXXV, 218-228.

Herklots, G. G. *Nathan Söderblom: Apostle of Christian Unity.* London: SCM Press, 1948.

Huntington, Henry S. "Archbishop Söderblom," *The Christian Century,* XLVIII, 946-948.

Johnson, William A. "Mystical and Revealed Religion in Nathan Söderblom," *Lutheran Quarterly,* XIV, 158-164.

Katz, Peter. *Nathan Söderblom: A Prophet of Christian Unity.* London: J. Clarke, 1946.

Nelson, Clifford Ansgar. "Nathan Söderblom, Prophet and Pioneer of Ecumenism," *Religion in Life,* XXXV, No. 5 (Winter, 1966), 774-788.

Pamp, Frederick D. "Archbishop Nathan Söderblom and Northfield," *Christendom,* LI, 123-124.

Sillen, Walter. "Nathan Söderblom and Christian Unity," *Christendom,* XII, 299-312.

——— "Nathan Söderblom," *The Journal of Religion,* XXVIII, 37-50.

Universal Council for Life and Work. *A Memorial to the First President of the Universal Christian Council for Life and Work.* Universal Council for Life and Work, 1931.

Visser 't Hooft, W. A. "Söderblom and the Roman Catholic Church," *The Christian Century,* XLIX, 617.

Westin, Gunnar. "Archbishop Söderblom and the Swedish Labor Movement," *Christendom,* V, 514-523.

Elson, W. P. "The Church that Made Archbishop Söderblom Great," *The Christian Century,* XLVIII, 1149.

Idleman, Finis. "Archbishop Söderblom," *The Christian Century,* XL, 1337-38.

Shillito, E. "Death of a Great Churchman," *The Christian Century,* XLVIII, 1003.

Acknowledgments

Grateful acknowledgment is hereby made for permission to quote from the following published works:

To Oxford University Press, London, for permission to quote from *The Church and Peace*, published in 1929 by Clarendon Press, *The Nature of Revelation*, published in 1933, and *The Living God*, published in 1933, all three by Nathan Söderblom.

To Morehouse-Barlow Company, Inc., New York, for permission to quote from *The Mystery of the Cross* by Nathan Söderblom, published 1933.

To the Christian Century Foundation, Chicago, for permission to quote from "Placet!" an editorial published in the December 22, 1965, issue of *The Christian Century*.

To Saint Xavier College, Chicago, for permission to quote from the article, "Teilhard de Chardin: A Philosophy of Procession," by E. R. Baltazar, published in the Spring 1964 issue of *Continuum*.

To Association Press, New York, for permission to quote from *The New Essence of Christianity* by William Hamilton, published 1961.

To Fleming H. Revell Company, Westwood, N.J., for permission to quote from *Christian Fellowship* by Nathan Söderblom, published 1923.

To Koehler & Amelang, Leipzig, for permission to quote from *Von der Kirche zur Welt* by Hanfried Müller, published 1961.

To the Macmillan Company for permission to quote from *The Secular City* by Harvey Cox, copyright Harvey Cox 1965, and *The Secular Meaning of the Gospel* by Paul M. van Buren, copyright Paul M. van Buren 1963.

To The Bobbs-Merrill Company, Inc., Indianapolis, for permission to quote from *Radical Theology and the Death of God*, copyright © 1966 by Thomas J. J. Altizer and William Hamilton.

To the Press Department of the U.S. Catholic Conference, Inc., Washington, for permission to quote from the Vatican Council documents *Declaration on the Relation of the Church to Non-Christian Religions*, English translation, 1965, and *Decree Concerning the Pastoral Office of Bishops in the Church*, English translation, 1965.

To Paulist Press (Paulist Fathers), Glen Rock, N.J., for permission to quote from *The Decree on Ecumenism of the Second Vatican Council,* A New Translation by the Secretariat for Promoting Christian Unity, copyright 1965 by The Missionary Society of St. Paul the Apostle in the State of New York.

To John Knox Press, Richmond, Va., for permission to quote from "Creative Negation in Theology," by Thomas J. J. Altizer, originally printed in the July 7, 1965, issue of *The Christian Century.* Reprinted in *Frontline Theology* (Richmond, Va.: John Knox Press, 1967).

To the *Official Register of Harvard University* for permission to quote from "The Sphere of Revelation" by Conrad Bergendoff, published in the April 25, 1949, issue of the *Harvard Divinity School Bulletin* (Number 14), *Official Register of Harvard University,* XLVI, No. 10.

To Charles Scribner's Sons, New York, for permission to quote from *The Philosophy of Religion* by Emil Brunner, published 1937.

To Harper & Row, Publishers, New York, for permission to quote from *The Phenomenon of Man,* by Pierre Teilhard de Chardin, the revised version, copyright 1965 by Harper & Row, Publishers, Inc.

Index